THE ADVANCE INTO KENTUCKY
PRIOR TO THE AMERICAN REVOLUTION

Frontier
Kentucky

Frontier Kentucky

OTIS K. RICE

THE UNIVERSITY PRESS OF KENTUCKY

Copyright © 1993 by The University Press of Kentucky

Scholarly publisher for the Commonwealth,
serving Bellarmine College, Berea College, Centre
College of Kentucky, Eastern Kentucky University,
The Filson Club, Georgetown College, Kentucky
Historical Society, Kentucky State University,
Morehead State University, Murray State University,
Northern Kentucky University, Transylvania University,
University of Kentucky, University of Louisville,
and Western Kentucky University.

Editorial and Sales Offices: Lexington, Kentucky 40508-4008

Library of Congress Cataloging-in-Publication Data

Rice, Otis K.
  Frontier Kentucky / Otis K. Rice.
     p.   cm.
  Includes bibliographical references and index.
  ISBN 0-8131-1840-9 (acid-free paper)
  1. Kentucky—History—To 1792. I. Title.
F454.R52 1993
976.9'02—dc20   93-7821

FOR MY KENTUCKY FAMILY

Sarah Lee & David Skaggs
Martha & Edwin Thomas

Contents

Preface

THE HISTORY of frontier Kentucky is an oft-told story, and in an account as brief as the present one there is certain to be much that is familiar to the informed Kentuckian. In this synthesis I have attempted to present the early history of Kentucky as a colorful and significant chapter in the expansion of the American frontier and as an important part of the development of the nation itself.

Essentially, I have dealt with four major themes. The first concerns the great imperial rivalry between England and France in the mid-eighteenth century for control of the Ohio Valley, of which Kentucky is a part. The outcome of that struggle was to have decisive influence upon the subsequent history of Kentucky. A second theme centers around the struggle of white settlers to possess lands claimed by the Indians and the liquidation of Indian rights through agreements such as the treaties of Hard Labor, Fort Stanwix, Lochaber, and Pittsburgh and through bloody conflicts such as Pontiac's uprising, Dunmore's War, and the Revolutionary War. Third, I have sought to deal with the importance of the land, the role of the speculator, and the progress of settlement. A fourth theme relates to the conquest of a wilderness bountiful in its riches but exacting in its demands and the planting of political, social, and cultural institutions.

Obviously, any attempt to provide specific dates for the frontier era of Kentucky history must involve a somewhat arbitrary decision, since vestiges of frontier life remained in many parts of the state for several generations. Partly because it was my original assignment for this series and partly because the end of the Revolutionary War seems to have been a rather significant point in the history of pioneer Kentucky, I have chosen to carry my account only to 1783. By then basic settlement patterns had emerged, the land system had been well established, the most pressing defense needs of the pioneers had been met, and the groundwork for political, social, and cultural institutions had been laid.

In any work, however brief, an author incurs debts. Nearly two decades ago Thomas D. Clark awakened my interest in the history of the American frontier and in the trans-Appalachian region in particular. I am also grateful to Mr. Neal O. Hammon of Louisville, Kentucky, and Mrs. May Wollerton of Montgomery, West Virginia, for sharing useful materials. My colleague Professor Stephen W. Brown of the History Department of West Virginia Institute of Technology has read the entire manuscript several times during the course of its preparation and, as usual, has been my best critic.

1

A Pawn on the
International Chessboard

For THOUSANDS of Americans George Caleb Bingham's famous painting of Daniel Boone leading an immigrant party through Cumberland Gap in the spring of 1775 has symbolized the opening of Kentucky and even of the trans-Appalachian West. Although Bingham's portrayal captures something of the glamor that always surrounds a daring adventurer, as well as of the optimism and buoyancy of the American frontier, no one work of art can explain the complex forces and circumstances behind such exciting moments of history.

The drama of frontier Kentucky had its beginnings a full century before the arrival of Boone, his predecessor James Harrod, and other immigrants. As part of the Ohio Valley, Kentucky was vitally affected by the international rivalry between England and France; both had laid claim to the region by the end of the third quarter of the seventeenth century. France based her rights upon the alleged discovery and exploration of the Ohio River by René-Robert Cavalier, sieur de la Salle, in 1669. English claims rested in part upon the Virginia charter of 1609, which described the boundaries of the colony as extending two hundred miles north and south of Old Point Comfort and westward from the Atlantic

Ocean to the Pacific. More specifically, England claimed the Ohio Valley by virtue of the discovery in 1671 of the New River, a remote tributary of the Ohio, by Thomas Batts and Robert Fallam. Sent out from Fort Henry on the Appomattox River by Abraham Wood, a prosperous fur trader, Batts and Fallam crossed the Blue Ridge and came upon the westward-flowing New, which they followed to Peters' Falls near the Virginia-West Virginia border. With appropriate ceremony they took possession for England of the lands drained by its waters and those into which the New River emptied.

Perhaps the first Virginian (or Englishman) to visit Kentucky was a member of another expedition sent out by Wood in 1673. Led by James Needham, its purpose was to open a direct trade with remote Indian tribes and thereby eliminate the profiteering by the Occaneechi middlemen with whom the traders of Virginia dealt. Needham made contacts with a tribe known as the To-mahittan, probably the Yuchi along the Hiwassee River. They proved friendly, and Needham left young Gabriel Arthur with them to learn their language and customs. During the winter of 1673–1674 Arthur accompanied the Indians on a military expedition against the Shawnees in Ohio. After a harrowing experience as a captive, Arthur was released and escorted by the Shawnees to the Warriors Path which led across the meadowlands of Kentucky to the Cumberland Gap and thence to the land of the Tomahittans.

For half a century the claims of England and France to the Ohio Valley lay dormant. Among the most powerful claimants were the Iroquois Indians, who established an overlordship of resident tribes during their conquests in the first half of the seventeenth century. In time the influence of the Iroquois over their subject tribes waned, but England, with whom the Iroquois were allied, continued to respect their claims. With interests best served by dealing directly with the tributary tribes, France refused to recognize any rights asserted by the Iroquois. British influence usually predominated as well with the Cherokees, who also claimed the part of the Ohio Valley south of the Ohio River. French fur traders from Canada and English traders from Virginia and Pennsylvania visited the region in ever-increasing numbers, and by the 1730s rivalry between them had reached a high intensity.

For France the Ohio Valley was important because it provided an essential link in communications between the provinces of Canada and Louisiana, which flanked her great crescent-shaped river empire in North America. To protect these communications, particularly the Maumee-Wabash route between Lake Erie and the Ohio River, France in the 1720s erected Forts Miami, Ouiatenon, and Vincennes. Scattered elsewhere throughout her vast wilderness empire, she built other posts, most of them small military enclaves tolerated by the Indian inhabitants out of mingled fear, respect, and economic advantage. These establishments gave France a position of primacy in the Ohio Valley.

By the beginning of King George's War in March 1744, English traders had begun to challenge French supremacy in the Ohio Valley. Financed by wealthy merchants, Pennsylvania traders crossed the Allegheny Mountains with pack trains of powder, lead, rum, hatchets, knives, and other desirable articles for which they obtained furs and hides from tribes along the Ohio and Allegheny rivers and on the southern shores of Lake Erie. Unfortunately for France, King George's War brought new problems. The British navy, which controlled the Atlantic Ocean, cut off supplies of trading goods to Canadian merchants and seriously disrupted French commerce with the Ohio Valley tribes. Seizing upon the trading vacuum thus created, Pennsylvania traders moved into the region and further drew the Indians away from their French attachments.

The king of the Pennsylvania traders was George Croghan, who had emigrated from Ireland during the

3

potato famine of 1741. Scarcely literate, possessed of poor judgment in business matters, and devious and deceptive in his dealings with others, Croghan was nevertheless noted for his consummate skill in winning and holding the trust and friendship of the Indians. No portrait of him is known to exist, but, as his major biographer points out, if one were available it would be "merely a disguise, a pleasing facade which aided him in his eighteenth-century confidence game." From his trading posts at Pine Creek, Logstown, and Beaver Creek, Croghan sent his men northward to the shores of Lake Erie, westward to the Wabash, and southward to the Kentucky River, including the Shawnee town of Eskippakithiki, near present Winchester, Kentucky. In 1748 he ordered the construction of a palisaded fort at the Miami village of Pickawillany in the very heart of the French trading country. In August of that year he and Conrad Weiser, a gentle Palatine Pietist knowledgeable in the ways of the Indians, lured the Delaware, Shawnee, Wyandot, and Iroquois chieftains to Logstown, where they pledged allegiance to England.

The Treaty of Aix-la-Chapelle, which brought King George's War, or the War of the Austrian Succession, to a close in 1748, left the situation in the Ohio Valley unresolved. Moreover, the indecisiveness of the conflict with respect to the great commercial struggle between England and France left little doubt that hostilities would ere long be resumed. Indeed, the diplomats had scarcely affixed their signatures to the treaty before influential English merchants, with the Duke of Newcastle and William Pitt as their principal political spokesmen, began to contend that peace was beneficial only to France. They urged prompt resumption of war against France as a means of destroying their commercial rival and enabling English merchants to reap the rewards of a profitable trade. Aggressive English colonial leaders and ardent expansionists, particularly in Virginia, welcomed the pressures exerted by English merchants upon the imperial government and found in them encouragement to pursue a more forward policy toward the Ohio Valley. The future of Kentucky rode on the outcome of these international conflicts.

The possibility of losing the fur trade of Kentucky and the region between the Ohio River and the Great Lakes troubled French and Canadian officials less than the threat to their trade north of the Great Lakes and to communications between Canada and Louisiana. In fact, in 1748 the Comte de la Galissioniere, the governor general of Canada, declared in a confidential report to his government that the economic value of the Ohio Valley to France was negligible. Her fur trade there had been steadily declining and the expense of maintaining posts was comparatively large. Nevertheless, political and strategic considerations made its retention imperative. Galissioniere, therefore, urged the French government to destroy the alarming influence of the English traders in the Ohio Valley and to bring the region firmly into the political and economic orbit of France.

Convinced that a display of force was necessary to regain the allegiance of the Ohio Valley Indians, Galissioniere dispatched an expedition of about 230 Canadian militia, Troupes de la Marine, Mission Iroquois, and Abenaki warriors into the Ohio country. Its leader was a Canadian, Pierre-Joseph Celoron de Blainville. Accompanying the expedition was Father Joseph-Pierre de Bonnecamps, whose duties included the preparation of maps and descriptive statements of the country through which it passed. Traveling southward from Fort Niagara, Blainville descended the Allegheny and Ohio rivers. Along the way he buried lead plates which bore inscriptions asserting the claim of France to the Ohio Valley. Although he was able to intimidate some of the English traders whom he encountered, he found the Indians singularly unimpressed and in some cases, as with the Miami at Pickawillany, decidedly hostile. Except for possible campsites on the south bank of the Ohio, their

5

journey did not carry the Frenchmen into Kentucky. The later discovery that they had missed the Big Bone Lick by only a few miles proved a source of profound disappointment to Father Bonnecamps.

Blainville's discouraging report of Indian defections and the domination of the Ohio Valley by English traders spurred French and Canadian officials to new action. Convinced that the French hold upon the region depended upon the support of the Indians, Governor General Ange de Menneville, the Marquis de Duquesne, in 1753 sent over two thousand Troupes de la Marine and Canadian militia to construct a road from Lake Erie to the headwaters of the Ohio and to erect forts at strategic points along the route. In charge of the operation he placed Captain Pierre-Paul de la Malgué, sieur de Marin, who, declared Duquesne, had been born with a tomahawk in his hand. So urgently did Marin press the work forward that he ruined his health and brought on his own death and that of nearly four hundred of his men. His energetic show of power, however, so affected the Indians that they began to sever their trading connections with the English. By the end of 1753 the English position in the Ohio Valley was shattered, and hardly a Pennsylvania or Virginia trader was left south of the Great Lakes.

Of far greater significance to the future of Kentucky were countermoves by the English, particularly the Virginians. The most promising of these actions appeared to be the extension to the trans-Appalachian region of the land system which had proved so successful in populating the Valley of Virginia after 1730. This plan had made use of speculators, who were granted one thousand acres of land for each family that they brought into the Valley. It had resulted in the settlement of large numbers of Germans and Scotch-Irish, with the latter being predominant in the southern parts of the Valley, from which many early Kentucky pioneers would be drawn.

Encouraged by the success of the Valley settlements in forming a buffer between the French and Indians and the valuable Piedmont plantations, Virginia land speculators, like the traders, were ready to challenge French claims to the trans-Allegheny region. Certainly with their approval, if not in their employ, John Howard, a resident of the South Branch of the Potomac River, in 1743 undertook a journey westward on "the Lakes & River of Mississippi." With him were John Peter Salling and three other men. They followed a circuitous route by way of the Greenbrier, New, Coal, and Kanawha rivers to the Ohio, where they constructed a bullboat. Aboard this crude craft, they traced the northern boundary of Kentucky for some five hundred miles and then continued down the Mississippi. Suspicious French officials placed them under arrest and took them to New Orleans. After almost two years Salling escaped and made his way back to Virginia, but Howard and the other members of the party were sent to France for trial. Salling undoubtedly provided information regarding transmontane Virginia for the famous map made by Joshua Fry and Peter Jefferson and first published in 1751.

Virginia speculators, no less than the English fur traders, saw a golden opportunity in the outbreak of King George's War. They were further encouraged by the Treaty of Lancaster, concluded with the Iroquois in July 1744. According to the interpretation of the agreement by Virginia officials, the Iroquois relinquished their claims to lands west of the Alleghenies and south of the Ohio, most of which lay in present Kentucky and West Virginia. No longer reluctant to grant lands beyond the mountains, the council of Virginia between 1745 and 1754 awarded more than 2.5 million acres to speculators on terms generally similar to those offered in the Valley of Virginia.

Because of the unsettled, and potentially explosive, international situation in the Ohio Valley, only three of

7

the speculative enterprises achieved even a modicum of success. With French power in the Ohio Valley then at its zenith, promoters of settlement west of the mountains could hope to achieve their goals only by forming strong combinations and by receiving support from the government of Virginia. Not surprisingly, the Greenbrier Company, which included members of the prominent Lewis family of Augusta County and whose lands in the Greenbrier Valley were within comparatively close proximity to the Valley of Virginia, enjoyed the greatest initial success. The other two combinations, the Loyal Company and the Ohio Company of Virginia, both of which played an important role in the early history of Kentucky, sought more remote lands and at times faced almost insurmountable obstacles.

Unquestionably the best known of the three speculative groups was the Ohio Company, formed in 1747 for the dual purpose of engaging in the Indian trade and planting settlements. Its membership consisted of several prominent Virginians, among whom were Thomas Lee, Augustine Washington, and George Fairfax, and the well-known Maryland frontier leader, Thomas Cresap. Adding an imperial dimension to its intercolonial character were the inclusion of Thomas Hanbury, an influential London merchant, to its membership and a directive of the British Board of Trade to a reluctant council of Virginia to make a grant of land to the company.

Yet, for all its prestige, the Ohio Company encountered serious obstacles. Foremost was the undisguised hostility of the government of Virginia, which questioned the right of the Board of Trade to dispose of territory granted the colony under its charter of 1609. In addition, ambiguities in the Treaty of Lancaster of 1744 gave rise to conflicting interpretations by the Iroquois and Virginia authorities with respect to the territory ceded by the Indians and made any advance into the Ohio Valley hazardous. Moreover, Pennsylvania traders vigorously opposed the entry of the company into the upper Ohio Valley and the settlement of families west of the Alleghenies. They resorted to a variety of stratagems to foil the company's plans and to dissuade the Indians from reaching any accommodation with Virginia. Finally, difficulties were also posed by the government of New York, which contested the right of Virginia to deal directly with the Iroquois.

In its petition for 500,000 acres of land west of the Alleghenies, the Ohio Company suffered another rebuff. Initially it was granted only 200,000 acres, in return for which it was required to settle one hundred families within seven years and to construct a fort in the Indian country. When it had complied with these stipulations, it might have an additional 300,000 acres on similar terms. The original portion of the grant was restricted to the area bounded by the Ohio and Kanawha rivers and the Allegheny Mountains, but later claims were made to Kentucky lands.

Undaunted as obstacle piled upon obstacle, the Ohio Company went ahead with its plans. It engaged the eminent North Carolina surveyor, Christopher Gist, to explore the Ohio Valley in search of lands suitable for settlement. It instructed Gist to gather information concerning routes of travel, rivers, mountain passes, the quality of the soil, and the Indian inhabitants. In addition, Gist carried invitations to the Indian chiefs to meet with Virginians at Logstown in 1752 for the purpose of drawing up a treaty of friendship.

Setting out from Thomas Cresap's residence at Old Town, Maryland, on October 31, 1751, Gist journeyed by way of the Susquehanna and Juniata rivers to Shannopin's Town. From there he continued to Logstown, where he embarked upon the Ohio. Farther down the Ohio he left the river and traveled by land to Pickawillany, where he began his descent of the Miami River to the Ohio. Gist undoubtedly had his eye upon Kentucky lands, but at the mouth of the Kentucky River he was

9

warned against proceeding on to the Falls of the Ohio because of danger from French-dominated Indians. Except for this friendly gesture, Gist found little encouragement from either Indians or fur traders in the Ohio country. His report convinced the Ohio Company that any move into the central Ohio Valley would be premature. Deciding, therefore, to confine its activities to the area set forth in the royal instructions, the company in 1752 dispatched Gist on a second expedition, which took him to the mouth of the Kanawha and into central West Virginia. The exploration of Kentucky must await a more propitious time.

Also interested in Kentucky was the Loyal Company, formed partly as a response to the directive of the Board of Trade with respect to the Ohio Company. Rankling under the assumption of authority over lands claimed by Virginia by the Board of Trade, John Robinson, the Speaker of the House of Burgesses, took the initiative in the organization of the Loyal Company. Other prominent members included John Lewis, Peter Jefferson, Joshua Fry, and Edmund Randolph. The generous terms accorded the company, which was granted 800,000 acres of land without the usual requirement that it seat one family for each thousand acres, reflected both the political influence of its members and Virginia's irritation with the Board of Trade.

On March 12, 1749, the Loyal Company employed Dr. Thomas Walker, a graduate of the College of William and Mary and a reputable surveyor, to locate tracts of land west of the Appalachians. The following year, on March 6, Walker and five companions set out from Walker's home near Charlottesville for the West. For the next four months they traversed the rugged country of southwestern Virginia, eastern Kentucky, and southern West Virginia. Part of the terrain was familiar to Walker, who had visited the Holston River country with James Patton in 1748. In his new expedition he explored the valleys of the Holston, Clinch, and Powell before reaching Cave Gap, the historic pass through the Cumberland Mountains.

Beyond the mountains Walker came upon a stream already known to hunters as the Shawnee River. Unaware that the river had been named, Walker called it the Cumberland in honor of the Duke of Cumberland, then a popular hero because of his victory over the English Jacobites in the battle of Culloden. In later times hunters gave the same name to the mountains and to the great pass through them.

On the northeast side of the Cumberland River, near present Barbourville, Kentucky, Walker and his men found a large bottom of fertile land. Leaving three men to build a cabin and plant a field of corn as a means of establishing a claim to the land, Walker and two companions continued to explore the surrounding country. About a week later Walker and his party, discouraged by the general unattractiveness of the region, turned homeward. Slowly they worked their way through the forests of eastern Kentucky to the Big Sandy River. From there they battled the rugged terrain of southern West Virginia to the Bluestone and New rivers. Then, by way of the Greenbrier Valley, where they found lands already settled, they crossed the Alleghenies and returned home.

For the moment prospects of an advance into Kentucky appeared dim. Tribal chiefs who gathered at Logstown in August 1752 agreed with considerable reluctance to some settlement on the upper Ohio, but the absence of an official representative of the Onondaga Council of the Iroquois made any agreement nearly meaningless. Nor was Pennsylvania represented at the council, and Pennsylvania traders were certain to try to block Virginia expansion beyond the Alleghenies. Of greater consequence was the success of Marin in fortifying the upper Ohio and in cementing French ties with the Ohio Valley tribes in 1753. Under these circumstances, the Ohio Company established only one settle-

11

ment before the French and Indian War. It was located at Redstone Old Fort on the Monongahela River and consisted of only eleven families. The Loyal Company confined its activities to the Holston and Clinch valleys. Conditions there were also unfavorable to the planting of settlements before the French and Indian War.

Viewing the French moves into the upper Ohio Valley as intolerable encroachments upon Virginia territory, Robert Dinwiddie, the aggressive Scottish governor of the colony, took imperial affairs into his own hands. In October 1753 he dispatched young George Washington to Fort Le Boeuf with a message to Jacques le Gardeur de Saint-Pierre, the French commandant in the Ohio Valley, calling upon the French to withdraw. The courtly Saint-Pierre received Washington with becoming dignity, but he declared that France had violated no agreements with England and that she would not leave the Ohio Valley.

By this time both the French and the Virginians had grasped the strategic value of the Forks of the Ohio. Upon Washington's recommendation, Dinwiddie in January 1754 ordered a construction crew of thirty-seven men to build a fort at the site. Duquesne, meanwhile, had decided to complete the French chain of posts and dispatched about five hundred troops and militia to construct the southernmost of the forts at the Forks of the Ohio. Although William Trent, who was in charge of the Virginia crew, had a fort well under way when the French arrived, he was forced by their overwhelming numbers to abandon his task, surrender the site to the French, and retire to Williamsburg.

Expecting a Virginia fort to be nearing completion, George Washington and about 150 men set out in April to serve as its garrison. Although he met the work party returning home, Washington decided to continue on. Warned of his approach, Claude-Pierre Pecaudy de Contrecoeur, who was in charge of the French forces at the Forks of the Ohio, instructed a party of thirty-three men under Ensign Joseph Coulon de Villiers de Jumonville to intercept Washington and demand that he leave. Washington, however, surrounded Jumonville's camp at night and, with about forty soldiers and a few Iroquois, launched a daybreak attack in which he forced the French to surrender. In the clash Jumonville was killed. Knowing that French retaliation was certain, Washington threw up a small defense, aptly called Fort Necessity. He was unable to cope with a superior French force, however, and had no alternative except to capitulate.

French power in the Ohio Valley following the confrontation at the Forks of the Ohio appeared formidable indeed. Earlier Charles-Michel Langlade had led a successful assault upon Pickawillany, and Contrecoeur had boasted that with Indian support he would drive the English from the transmontane area. Now the last vestiges of Indian attachment to the British melted away, and the French had command of the Ohio River from its source to its mouth. They and their Indian allies were capable of striking at the rear of the English colonies almost at will.

With the shedding of blood in the Ohio Valley, Dinwiddie addressed an urgent appeal to England for regular troops. His call, echoed in other colonies, gave support to the war party in England, which, led by the Duke of Cumberland, Henry Fox, and William Pitt, forced the Duke of Newcastle to agree to a full-scale military operation against the French in the Ohio Valley without a formal declaration of war. In April 1755 Major General Edward Braddock arrived in Virginia with two regiments of British Regulars. With colonial militia and Indian guides to bring his army to nearly two thousand men, he advanced upon Fort Duquesne, the French post at the Forks of the Ohio. Within a few miles of his destination he was surprised by about 250 Troupes de la Marine and Canadian militia and some six hundred Indians under Captain Daniel Beaujeu. The French killed or captured two-thirds of Braddock's army, with a loss of only twenty-three men killed and twenty wounded. Worse yet, the captured baggage of Braddock, who was among those killed, contained plans for British campaigns on other fronts and enabled the French to foil them.

Although war had not yet been declared, the governor general of New France, Pierre-François de Rigaud, Marquis de Vaudreuil-Cavagnal, took the offensive and sent Indian war parties, many of them led by Canadian officers, against the Virginia and Pennsylvania frontiers, where they spread death and destruction. Essentially a defensive strategy, his plan was to hold the Indian tribes firmly in alliance with the French in order to offset superior British numbers. This strategy would compel the latter to commit large forces to the defense of the frontiers and to draw further upon their manpower for building roads and maintaining supply lines. Conversely, with their command of the inland rivers, the French could move men and supplies with comparative ease.

The Indian raids into the Virginia backcountry provided Kentucky with its first known woman visitor, albeit an unwilling one. In their attack upon the settlement at Draper's Meadows, on New River, near present Blacksburg, Virginia, the Indians took as one of their captives Mary Ingles, the wife of a prominent settler. When they were only three days from her home, Mrs. Ingles gave birth to a child, but she chose to continue with her captors rather than face certain death should she remain behind. After several weeks of captivity, she was taken by the Indians to the Big Bone Lick in Kentucky, where they made salt. While they were there, Mrs. Ingles and an elderly Dutch, or German, woman contrived to escape. After a heart-rending decision to leave Mrs. Ingles's young infant behind, they made their way to the Ohio River and followed its south bank to the mouth of the Kanawha. Keeping to the Kanawha,

14

they at last reached the New River and the Ingles home, but not before fatigue, hunger, and exposure had produced a temporary mental derangement in the Dutch woman during which she threatened to kill and eat Mrs. Ingles.

Mary Ingles's return home with information that the Shawnee warriors were then in their towns undoubtedly contributed to the decision of Governor Dinwiddie to authorize the Big Sandy River, or Sandy Creek, Expedition, the only military movement of the French and Indian War to touch Kentucky soil. With settlers from the upper Potomac southward to the Greenbrier and New River valleys pleading for protection and the promise of the Cherokees to provide 150 warriors for a campaign against the Shawnees, Dinwiddie had no alternative except to order a move into the Indian country. The expedition, which held its rendezvous at Fort Frederick, near Ingles Ferry on New River, was under the command of Major Andrew Lewis, a thirty-five-year-old veteran of the Braddock campaign and an officer with a reputation as an excellent disciplinarian. Altogether, it consisted of about 340 men, of whom between 80 and 130 were Cherokees.

Hastily organized and inadequately provisioned, the expedition experienced nothing but hardship and disappointment from the time that it left Fort Frederick on February 18, 1756. Torrential rains, flooded streams, scarcity of game, the loss of their supplies, and the collapse of their packhorses were but a few of the difficulties the men encountered. By early March their morale was at rock bottom. Desertions began to occur, and all Lewis's urgings that the expedition continue were in vain. The failure of the move opened the Virginia frontiers to new terrors, and even the defection of the Cherokees was threatened until Lewis constructed Fort Loudoun on the Holston for their protection.

Not until 1758, after William Pitt had invigorated the British war effort with new energy, did the situation in the Ohio Valley begin to change. Along with offensive moves against such powerful French positions as Louisbourge and Quebec, the British strategy called for an assault upon Fort Duquesne by Brigadier General John Forbes. Weakened by a shortage of supplies, the withdrawal of troops for other fighting fronts, and mass Indian defections after the Treaty of Easton of 1758, François Le Marchand de Ligneris, the commandant at Fort Duquesne, was in no position to repel an assault. He, therefore, removed the cannon, blew up the fort, and retired up the Allegheny River.

The occupation of the Forks of the Ohio and the construction of Fort Pitt at that site by the British broke the French power in the Ohio Valley. Although fighting continued on other fronts for another four years, the French and Indian War, for practical purposes, was over in the western country. The Treaty of Paris, which in 1763 ended the great conflict, transferred French possessions in North America to England. After fifteen years of uncertainty the Ohio Valley was English, and the national character, at least, of Kentucky had been determined.

Land speculators and prospective settlers who expected the conclusion of the French and Indian War to bring an immediate opening of the trans-Appalachian region were to suffer angry and bitter disappointment. Two events of 1763 pushed the advance into Kentucky into the not too distant but nevertheless unforeseeable future. One was the royal proclamation of October 7, which forbade settlement west of the Appalachian Mountains; the other was Pontiac's uprising.

The Proclamation of 1763 had its origins in part in the Treaty of Easton of 1758 and in a supplementary proclamation by Colonel Henry Bouquet in 1761. The Treaty of Easton, between the Iroquois and Sir William Johnson, acting in behalf of Pennsylvania, closed trans-Allegheny Pennsylvania to settlement and confirmed it to the Indians as a hunting ground. Interpreting impe-

16

rial approval of the treaty as acceptance of the principle of forbidding settlement west of the mountains, Bouquet, the commandant at Fort Pitt, extended its provisions to Maryland and Virginia.

Settlers and speculators fought tooth and nail against these blows to their expectations. The Ohio Company, whose aspirations reached to Kentucky, appealed to London to set aside the restrictions. Francis Fauquier, the governor of Virginia, himself laid the rights of the Greenbrier and Loyal companies before the Board of Trade. Professing a lack of sufficient knowledge to render "any explicit Opinion," the Board of Trade, however, enjoined the governor to take no action which might "in any degree, have a tendency" to excite the Indians. Meanwhile, several ranking military officers in Virginia, including George Mercer and George Washington, made it clear that they would "leave no stone unturned" in their efforts to acquire lands set aside by Governor Dinwiddie in 1754 for volunteers in the military forces of Virginia. While speculators were evincing such determination to obtain the forbidden lands, settlers were streaming across the mountains in defiance of agreements with the Indians and royal edict.

The determination of speculators and settlers to occupy the transmontane regions was directly responsible for Pontiac's uprising. Led by Pontiac, an Ottawa chief, the Indians sought to retain their homes and hunting grounds by striking at the British before they could fully recover from nine long years of debilitating conflict with the French. On May 7 Pontiac attacked Detroit, which held out against a prolonged siege, but other British posts, including Forts Joseph, Miami, Ouiatenon, and Michilimackinac, fell to Indian attackers in less than a month. At Bushy Run Bouquet defeated Shawnee, Delaware, Mingo, and Huron warriors who had besieged Fort Pitt and broke the power of the Indians on the upper Ohio. As reverses for the Indians continued and anticipated French assistance failed to materialize, Pon-

17

tiac's allies became discouraged, and one by one they capitulated to the British. Pontiac was the last to do so, holding out until 1765, when he met George Croghan at Fort Ouiatenon and agreed to end hostilities.

With the defeat of Pontiac, prospective settlers and speculators again allowed their hopes of advancing into the trans-Appalachian region to soar. There yet remained, however, the British restriction upon settlement west of the mountains. For the moment Kentucky, already becoming a land of legendary attractions, remained a forbidden territory known but to a few daring men.

2

The Realm of the Indian and the Hunter

Kᴇɴᴛᴜᴄᴋʏ in the mid-eighteenth century was a land of fabled beauty and indeterminate dimensions. In earliest usage the name was applied to a somewhat vague region extending westward from the Appalachian Mountains perhaps to the Mississippi River and southward from the Ohio to the homeland of the Cherokees in Tennessee. In its pristine state this vast domain was covered with great forests of oak, hickory, walnut, ash, poplar, beech, cucumber, and maples, among which were mingled stately evergreens. These forests were broken by clear-flowing streams and traversed by numerous ancient Indian trails.

The first visitors to Kentucky beheld in its beauty an almost infinite variety. Those entering by way of the Ohio River found south of that stream great canebrakes, where stalks sometimes grew to heights of twelve feet. Here, in their incessant struggles for Kentucky, Indian tribes had fought some of their deadliest battles. Farther to the west was an extensive grassland, six thousand square miles in area. These "Barrens" had been cleared of trees by the Indians, who hoped that grass might grow there and attract the vast herds of buffalo that roamed the prairies to the west.

Pioneers who reached Kentucky by way of Cumberland Gap encountered first the mountainous eastern section of the state. Toward the west the mountains diminished in height and ruggedness before giving way to a rolling plain, much of it covered with the famed Kentucky bluegrass and dotted with venerable trees. Nearly all who gazed upon the Bluegrass country described it in superlatives. John Filson, who with florid hyperbole entrenched a legendary Daniel Boone in the saga of the American frontier, in words worthy of that intrepid pioneer, depicted Kentucky as "the best tract of land in North-America, and probably in the world." Felix Walker found that in Kentucky "nature, in the profusion of her bounty, had spread a feast for all that lives." Walker must have captured the emotions of thousands of others as they first beheld the Bluegrass when he wrote, "We felt ourselves as passengers through a wilderness just arrived at the fields of Elysium, or at a garden where there was no forbidden fruit." He found the sight "so delightful to our view and grateful to our feelings" that he, like Columbus upon reaching the shores of the Bahamas, was moved to kiss the soil beneath him.

For nearly a decade after the Proclamation of 1763 most of the region west of the Appalachians remained the preserve of the Indians and of that colorful breed of men known as the Long Hunters. The Long Hunter did not suddenly burst upon the western forest. Even before Thomas Walker made his famous journey into Kentucky in 1750, hunters had been on the headwaters of the Tennessee and one had given his name to the Clinch River. Once the Ohio Valley Indians had made their peace with the English in the Treaty of Easton and subsequent understandings, hunters began to cross the mountains. In 1761 John and Samuel Pringle deserted the garrison at Fort Pitt for the Tygart Valley, a tributary of the Monongahela, where they hunted and trapped for several years. During that time they lived in a large hollow sycamore tree. Soon afterward John Simpson set up a camp on the West Fork of the Monongahela near present Clarksburg, West Virginia. Before the end of the 1760s scores of hunters, who usually banded together in relatively large parties, were crossing the Cumberlands into eastern and central Tennessee.

In no part of the transmontane region did the Long Hunters play a more significant role than in Kentucky. The first party to point the way from the Holston Valley to Kentucky set out in 1761 under the leadership of Elisha Walden, a "rough backwoodsman" then about thirty years old. He and the eighteen or nineteen men with him established their base of operations, or station camp, where they stored skins and supplies, on Wallen's Creek, in present Lee County, Virginia. For eighteen months they remained in the region between Long Island in the Holston and Cumberland Gap. In 1763, with many of the same men, Walden undertook another extensive hunting expedition, this time passing through Cumberland Gap into southeastern Kentucky. The hunters then moved on to the Rockcastle River country and visited Crab Orchard, later a prominent point on the Wilderness Road.

In many ways Walden's men were typical of others who hunted in Kentucky for extended periods. Clothed in coonskin or otter caps, buckskin moccasins and leggings, and long hunting shirts of soft leather and equipped with hatchets and hunting knives, they, no less than the Indians, were well prepared for the wilderness. Like other Long Hunters, they constructed a half-faced camp, built of poles, covered with puncheons, and enclosed on three sides. Because large groups frightened the game and attracted the attention of Indians, they usually hunted in parties of three or four. The latter often ranged many miles from the station camp and returned only to store their pelts or to obtain supplies. At the station camp furs and skins were guarded from hungry wolves and bears by placing them on pole scaffolds built several feet above the ground and protected from the weather by covering them with elk or buffalo hides or with strips of peeled bark. Once they had completed their work, the hunters folded their pelts and packed them in bales weighing from fifty to a hundred pounds, two of which were carried by each packhorse on the homeward journey.

Seeking to emulate the success of Walden's expedition, other hunters probed deep into the Kentucky wilderness. Their favorite trail was one which led them westward by way of Cumberland Gap and the Warriors Path. They crossed the Cumberland River at a ford at present Pineville, Kentucky, and went from there to the mouth of Stinking Creek, some eight miles distant. Once they had reached that point, they scattered in various directions into the country along the Dix and Rockcastle rivers and even to the Green River. Most expeditions were organized after the crops had been harvested, but no season was without its hunting parties.

Scores of riflemen, some of whose journeys have been lost to history, sought the fur regions of Kentucky and Tennessee. In 1766 James Smith of western Pennsylvania and four companions took the route through Cumberland Gap to the waters of the Cumberland and the Tennessee. Smith had been for twenty-four years a captive of the Indians and had probably traversed parts of Kentucky many times. One of the most noted of the expeditions was that led by Benjamin Cutbird of North Carolina. Cutbird crossed the Appalachians by a little-known Indian trail. His party hunted across southern Kentucky and northern Tennessee to the Mississippi River and descended that stream to New Orleans, where Cutbird sold his furs.

Other hunters entered Kentucky from the west. Half a century before the English began to penetrate the region beyond the Cumberland Gap, Frenchmen from the Illinois settlements were hunting along the lower Ohio. Unlike the English, French hunters traveled by water and confined their activities to lands along the rivers and their tributaries. There deer and buffalo fed on the cane which grew along the streams, and hunters could easily kill animals within carrying distance of their pirogues. Among the favorite areas of the French hunters were the valleys of the Cumberland, then known as the Shawnee, and Green rivers.

The entry of the Philadelphia firm of Baynton, Wharton, and Morgan into the trade of the Illinois country in 1766 introduced a new element into hunting in western Kentucky. Domesticated animals were so scarce in the Illinois settlements that young George Morgan, the firm's representative, had to depend upon wild meat, particularly the buffalo, for food. When the supply of game along the lower Ohio was exhausted, Morgan sent hunters into the Cumberland Valley, one of whom, Jacques Thimote De Monbruen, ascended the river as far as present Nashville. Other hunters covered much of the region along the Cumberland and Green rivers.

In 1768 Morgan planned to send out a band of some sixty hunters in four boats. At least two of the boats departed, and some of the men may have reached present Cumberland County, Kentucky. The presence of Morgan's hunters angered the Cherokees and Chickasaws, who generally did not mind their pursuing the buffalo but who opposed their taking deer and beaver. Young Simon Girty, one of the hunters, reported one attack by about thirty Indians in which only Girty was known to have escaped. Morgan believed that the attacks were inspired by the French, and possibly by the Spanish. The previous year James Harrod and George Michael Holsteiner, better known as Michael Stoner, both from the Fort Pitt area, crossed Kentucky from the Illinois settlements in a venture that carried them as far south as Nashville, but there is no evidence that they were employed by Morgan.

The year 1769 was a notable one in the annals of the Long Hunters in Kentucky as well as in the trans-Appalachian region generally. One of the largest parties left Fort Chiswell, on New River, in early June, with men drawn from the New River section of Virginia, Rockbridge County, and the Yadkin Valley of North Carolina. Among the leaders were such experienced hunters as Kasper Mansker, Uriah Stone, Richard Skaggs, and Abram and Isaac Bledsoe. Traveling by way of Walden's trail down Powell Valley, they crossed Cumberland Gap and then followed the Warriors Path to Flat Lick, Kentucky. From there they continued westward along the Cumberland River before turning southward into Tennessee. In the same year Hancock Taylor of Orange County, Virginia, led an expedition of hunters and explorers into Kentucky during the course of which he and several others launched a boat and journeyed to New Orleans.

In 1770 many of the hunters who had participated in the great party of the previous year returned to Kentucky and established a station camp on the Green River. From there they scattered throughout the watershed of that stream and into the Barrens. One group, led by James Knox of Augusta County, Virginia, left the main party and hunted on the Rockcastle River. While there the men met Captain Dick, a Cherokee chief, who told them that they would find plenty of game on "his river." Knox and his men located the stream described by the chief and named it Dick's (now spelled Dix) River in his honor.

The best known of all the Kentucky Long Hunters, and, indeed, of all those who hunted and trapped in the trans-Appalachian region for extended periods, was Daniel Boone. The Boone family had been in the large Scotch-Irish migration from Pennsylvania into the Valley of Virginia during the mid-eighteenth century. Like many other relative latecomers, it had pressed on to the southern extremities of the Great Valley and then turned eastward to the Yadkin Valley in North Carolina. There Daniel settled with his young wife, Rebecca, and a rapidly increasing family. Typical of that class referred to by Frederick Jackson Turner as pioneer farmers, Daniel was possessed of a restless nature that did not allow sustained attention to agricultural and domestic pursuits and which, instead, found fulfillment only in hunting and trapping and in an incurable wanderlust.

Boone first heard of the attractions of Kentucky from John Finley, whom he first met when both were teamsters with Braddock's expedition in 1755. At that time Finley told Boone of his experiences as an Indian trader in the Ohio Valley before the French and Indian War. Finley's account of his visit, as a captive, to Eskippakithiki, the Shawnee village near present Winchester, Kentucky, and his descriptions of the beauty and fertility of Bluegrass Kentucky left an indelible impression upon Boone. Finley's accounts of Kentucky were confirmed by reports of hunters who visited the region during the following decade.

In the spring of 1769, when Boone's longing to see the Bluegrass region was becoming almost overwhelming, fate itself seemed to intervene. Finley, now a peddler of household wares, journeyed into the Yadkin country and again met Boone, whom he had not seen in nearly fourteen years. A gifted raconteur, Finley once more related his experiences and extolled the meadowlands of Kentucky for their beauty and their abundance of game. His accounts lost nothing in the retelling, and Boone's determination to visit this elysium now became irrepressible.

Fired with excitement and anticipation, Boone and Finley set out for Kentucky on May 1, 1769. With them were John Stuart, Boone's brother-in-law, who had been a member of Cutbird's party, Joseph Holden, James Mooney, and William Cooley. Much of the territory covered in the first part of their journey was familiar to Boone, who had previously hunted in southwestern Virginia, the rugged Big Sandy Valley, and in the rough, laurel-covered hills of eastern Kentucky. Their route now carried them by way of Moccasin Gap to the Clinch·

25

Valley and then across Walden's Ridge of Powell Mountain into Powell Valley. The formidable Cumberland Mountain range deflected their course southwestward into a region of canebrakes, extensive meadows, and rolling timberlands.

As Boone and his companions approached Kentucky, they saw striking evidence of the impact of the Treaty of Hard Labor and were forcefully reminded that the future of Kentucky belonged to the settler rather than the hunter. A hundred miles beyond the outermost settlements on the Holston they unexpectedly came upon about twenty men busily at work erecting cabins, clearing lands, and planting corn. With Joseph Martin of Albemarle County, Virginia, as their leader, they had arrived a few weeks previously and were taking up tracts for Thomas Walker, who had visited the region nearly twenty years before in search of lands for the Loyal Company. Martin's Station, as the settlement came to be known, was to prove an important supply center for pioneers who later followed the Wilderness Road to Kentucky.

Once they were through the Cumberland Gap, Boone and his party crossed the divide between the Cumberland and Tennessee rivers to Yellow Creek and followed a path which led them to an old Indian camping ground at Flat Lick. From there they took the trail blazed by Walden and other hunters to the Rockcastle River. They then turned northward and emerged from the mountains near Big Hill, from which they gazed upon the great levels of Kentucky. From a camp set up on Red Lick Fork of Station Creek they explored the surrounding country. They were struck by the sight of great herds of buffalo, sometimes numbering in the hundreds, which grazed upon the cane leaves and natural grasses and sought the numerous salt springs of the region.

Boone's party had hardly arrived in the Bluegrass before it became acutely aware of unrelinquished claims of Indian tribes to lands south of the Ohio River. At Eskippakithiki, which Finley had visited fifteen years before, they found the remains of the last Indian village in Kentucky, reluctantly abandoned by the Shawnees, who had not surrendered any rights to Kentucky lands. Nor had the Cherokees, who had ceded territory by the Treaty of Hard Labor, at that time given up any part of Kentucky. While Boone and Stuart were hunting along the Kentucky River, they were captured by an Indian hunting party, but after seven days they managed to escape. They returned to their camp to find it plundered and Finley and the others gone home. Undaunted by this double blow, Boone and Stuart continued their hunting for several more weeks. Fearing for the safety of the two lone hunters, Boone's brother Squire and Alexander Neeley set out in search of them. Happily, they found Boone and Stuart, and the four remained to hunt and trap throughout the ensuing winter and into the next spring.

The small party was soon again reduced to two. While hunting alone, Stuart was killed by Indians, and Neeley became homesick and returned to the settlements. The indomitable Boones remained. When supplies ran low, Squire returned to North Carolina with their furs and obtained needed provisions, fresh horses, and ammunition. Left alone in the wilderness, Daniel ranged over a vast territory, going as far north as the Ohio, west to the falls of that river, and into the fertile valleys of the Kentucky and Licking rivers. On July 27, 1770, Squire rejoined Daniel at their old camp. The brothers then set out for the Cumberland and the southern part of Kentucky, where they spent the winter of 1770–1771. There, one early spring day of 1771, the seasoned hunter Kasper Mansker came upon Boone, who in the lonely wilds of Kentucky was singing at the top of his voice. His song, however, was so discordant that Mansker advanced toward him with great stealth in the belief that it might be some kind of Indian decoy.

At last, in March 1771, Daniel and Squire packed their furs and skins on their horses and began the journey homeward. For more than two years Daniel had been in Kentucky and had become more intimately acquainted with the region than any other man. Familiarity had inspired affection, and he made up his mind to move his family to Kentucky as soon as conditions permitted. Unfortunately for Boone's financial situation, he and Squire were intercepted at Cumberland Gap by a small band of Cherokees, who took their guns, horses, and pelts and ordered them to leave the western country. Daniel thus arrived home no richer than when he left.

Not long after the Boones departed, Simon Kenton, another noted hunter and scout, first arrived in Kentucky. The sixteen-year-old Kenton was a refugee, who had fled from eastern Virginia in the mistaken belief that he had killed a rival in a love affair. With two companions, probably George Yeager and Adam Strader, Kenton hunted for two years in the vicinity of Maysville, Kentucky, and along the Kanawha and Little Kanawha rivers. In 1773, while the three were hunting at the mouth of the Elk River, or present Charleston, West Virginia, Yeager, an experienced woodsman and mentor of Kenton, was killed by Indians. The following year Kenton served as a scout in Dunmore's War. After that conflict he returned to the Maysville region. In the summer of 1775 he joined the new settlement at Boonesborough, Kentucky, and in subsequent years he became one of the most distinguished Indian scouts. He participated in George Rogers Clark's expedition to the Illinois country in 1778, the raid against the Shawnees at Chillicothe later that year, and Anthony Wayne's campaign against the Indians in 1794. Like Boone, Kenton never mastered a restless spirit. Careless of legal matters, such as all-important land titles, he spent his last years in poverty.

Colorful and exciting as it was, the day of the Long

Hunter was brief. Rejecting any thought that the territory west of the central Appalachians should remain a permanent Indian domain, land speculators and prospective settlers kept a steady pressure upon British and colonial officials to shift the Proclamation line westward. Lord Shelburne, the Secretary of State for the Southern Department, which had charge of American colonial affairs, responded to their representations on January 5, 1768, by authorizing the delineation of a new boundary. On March 12 Lord Hillsborough, who assumed the post of Secretary of State for the American Department following a reorganization of the cabinet, directed Sir William Johnson and John Stuart, the Indian superintendents for the northern and southern departments, respectively, to open negotiations with the Indians for a revision of the Proclamation line.

Hillsborough gave Johnson and Stuart explicit instructions concerning the location of the new boundary. From the Susquehanna River, it was to run westward to the Ohio, follow that stream to the mouth of the Kanawha, and then follow a straight line to Chiswell's mine on New River. The new boundary would secure a 200,000-acre military grant promised by Governor Robert Dinwiddie to Virginians who had served in the French and Indian War and repeatedly demanded since that time by the House of Burgesses. It would also clear lands claimed by the Greenbrier Company, the original area from which the Ohio Company was to locate its lands, and part of the territory in which the Loyal Company was interested. Sir William Johnson was charged with arranging a treaty with the Iroquois and subsidiary tribes to cover lands north of the mouth of the Kanawha, and John Stuart was instructed to negotiate an agreement with the Cherokees for lands south of that point.

Even before the councils with the Indians began, Virginia speculators were expressing dissatisfaction with the line set forth by Hillsborough. Reflecting their ambitions, Stuart proposed to Hillsborough that the southern part of the line extend from Chiswell's mine to the mouth of the Kentucky rather than to the confluence of the Kanawha and the Ohio. The boundary suggested by Stuart would have satisfied the most extreme claims of the Loyal Company, provided adequate tracts for veterans of the French and Indian War, and allowed the Ohio Company, should its claims be recognized, to select from choice lands beyond the area originally prescribed for its grant. Stuart, however, found Hillsborough unyielding with respect to any further westward extension of the Indian boundary. Bowing to the secretary's dictate, Stuart gathered the Cherokee chiefs at Hard Labor Creek in South Carolina. The delineation of the boundary approved by the Treaty of Hard Labor on October 17, 1768, left the Cherokee claims to Kentucky intact and proved a complete disappointment to Virginia speculators.

The line agreed upon at Hard Labor was undermined by the Treaty of Fort Stanwix, which Sir William Johnson concluded with the Iroquois on November 5, 1768. When it appeared that a redefinition of the northern boundary was likely, representatives of powerful speculators called upon Johnson at his residence at New London, where they found him receptive to their overtures. The "Suffering Traders," composed of George Croghan, Joseph Galloway, Benjamin Franklin, Governor William Franklin of New Jersey, and the powerful Philadelphia business firms of Baynton, Wharton, and Morgan and Simon, Trent, Levy, and Franks, proved especially adept at getting the ear of the Indian superintendent. Samuel Wharton, William Trent, and George Croghan, who acted as spokesmen, alleged that the Pennsylvania traders had lost goods valued at £86,912 during Pontiac's uprising as a result of their efforts to establish business relations with residents of the Illinois country and western Indian tribes. As early as 1764 Croghan had begun to draw the traders together and, with the support of Johnson and General Thomas Gage, had

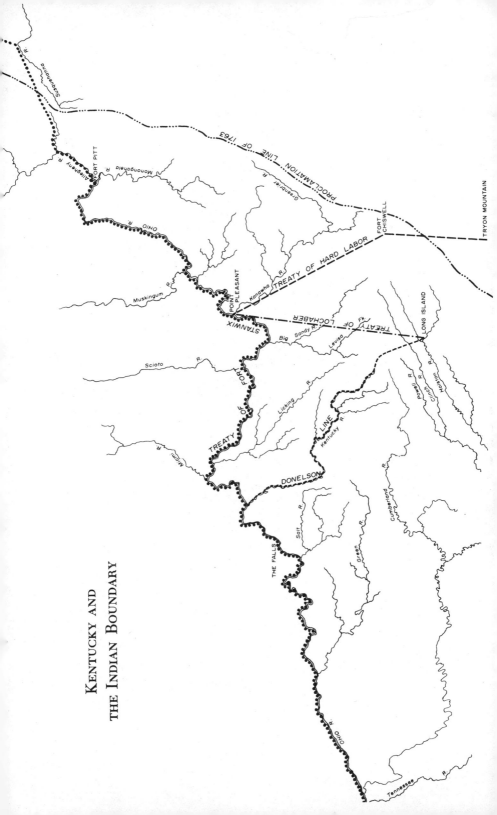

KENTUCKY AND
THE INDIAN BOUNDARY

launched the Illinois Company, which sought a grant of 1.2 million acres of land along the Mississippi as compensation for their losses. Now the Suffering Traders pinned their hopes on a private cession by the Iroquois, which might be recognized in the anticipated settlement with the Indians. In addition, Croghan hoped to secure recognition of a 200,000-acre grant near Fort Pitt and on the Youghiogheny River, which the Indians had first made to him in 1747.

Assured of Johnson's sympathy, Wharton and Trent visited the Iroquois in the summer of 1768 in an effort to obtain a prior commitment to a special grant for the Suffering Traders. What inducement they offered the Indians is not known, but if the Iroquois were to be forced to relinquish their lands they could hardly have had much concern about the recipients. Therefore, Wharton and Trent faced no formidable task.

A far greater obstacle in the path of the Suffering Traders lay in the fact that any lands granted them by the Iroquois were also within the boundaries of Virginia. For that reason Wharton and Trent discussed their proposals with Andrew Lewis and Thomas Walker, who were at that time Virginia's commissioners in the Mohawk country. Anticipating difficulty in obtaining any recognition of a private grant by Virginia, they apparently struck a bargain with Lewis and Walker. Incontrovertible evidence is lacking, but Lewis and Walker appear to have agreed to place no obstacle in the path of a grant to the merchants provided the Iroquois could be persuaded to cede lands as far west as the mouth of the Tennessee rather than to the mouth of the Kanawha, as Johnson's instructions specified. The additional territory would clear lands desired by the Loyal and Ohio companies and open desirable tracts for the Virginia military grant. Moreover, a large cession by the Iroquois would exert pressure upon John Stuart to obtain similar concessions from the Cherokees. In the light of subsequent events, the conclusion that some quid pro quo existed

32

between the Pennsylvanians and the Virginia commissioners is almost inescapable.

The Treaty of Fort Stanwix, not surprisingly, involved gross violations of the instructions Johnson had received from Hillsborough. To the traders, now styling themselves the Indiana Company, it awarded a large tract in present West Virginia, bounded by Laurel Hill, the Little Kanawha River, the Ohio, and the present southern border of Pennsylvania. The treaty also recognized the grant made to Croghan in 1747. Finally, as Lewis and Walker desired, the Iroquois gave up their rights to lands as far west as the mouth of the Tennessee River. As the ally of Virginia and Pennsylvania speculators, Johnson had thus negotiated the surrender of Iroquois claims to nearly all of Kentucky.

Once again, however, the future of Kentucky became involved in the intricacies and pressures of British politics. Lord Hillsborough and the Board of Trade condemned Johnson's deviation from his instructions. In May 1769 Hillsborough refused to approve the grant to the Indiana Company unless Johnson could offer a satisfactory explanation for the transaction. In addition, he instructed Johnson to refuse acceptance of the cession of lands west of the mouth of the Kanawha if the Indian superintendent could do so without offending the Indians. Johnson continued to assert that the Iroquois insisted upon conveying their rights to lands south of the Ohio to the British. Even if the Iroquois cession must be recognized in its entirety, Hillsborough warned Johnson, the Crown had no intention of permitting settlement beyond the mouth of the Kanawha. Not to be countenanced was any movement of population into Kentucky.

Speculators who hoped that the terms of the Treaty of Fort Stanwix might force a revision of the boundary established by the Treaty of Hard Labor were not disappointed. In response to their demands, Lord Botetourt, who had recently embarked upon his duties as governor of Virginia, asked Thomas Walker and Andrew Lewis to discuss an alteration in the southern portion of the line with John Stuart. The two Virginians achieved only modest success. The resulting Treaty of Lochaber of October 17, 1770, provided a new line extending from the North Carolina-Virginia border to a point near Long Island in the Holston River and running from there in a straight course to the mouth of the Kanawha. This boundary presumably struck a balance between the desire of the Virginia speculators, particularly the Loyal Company, for additional territory and the need to reassure the Cherokees, who feared occupation of their Kentucky hunting grounds. Nevertheless, the agreement was far from satisfactory to the Virginia speculators, and they immediately set about to obtain a more favorable boundary.

Adjustments to the line laid down by the Treaty of Lochaber led to extralegal moves and direct negotiation with the Cherokees. In the spring of 1771 John Donelson set out with a party of surveyors from Long Island in the Holston. Instead of proceeding to the mouth of the Kanawha, Donelson took a more northwesterly course. He and his men blamed this deviation from the prescribed line upon faulty instruments, but it seems more likely that Donelson knew what he was about and that he had succumbed to the persuasions of powerful speculators. When the surveyors reached a stream which they believed to be the Levisa Fork of the Big Sandy, Donelson prevailed upon the Cherokees who accompanied him to accept that river rather than the line specified in the treaty as the boundary. The stream, however, proved to be the Kentucky River rather than the west branch of the Big Sandy. The inaccurate maps of the day obscured the enormity of the error, and Stuart reluctantly agreed to the new line. By this time Stuart probably realized the futility of opposing the speculators; but he also hoped, apparently, that approval of the additional territory might postpone for some time any further controversies with the Indians.

With settlers and speculators impatiently awaiting every extension of the Indian boundary westward, the days when the Long Hunters reigned in the trans-Appalachian forests were numbered. Like the mountain men of the Rocky Mountains in the 1820s and 1830s, the Long Hunters traversed and became intimately acquainted with great expanses of territory during their brief era. Unlike most of the mountain men, many of them were experienced farmers, whose trained eyes sought out and carefully appraised lands suited to agriculture, not only for themselves but also for speculators. As early as 1764 Daniel Boone was locating lands for his friend and creditor, Richard Henderson, a judge of a North Carolina district court. Boone also spied out lands for Henderson during his extended expedition of 1769–1771. Henry Scaggs, another of the Long Hunters, served Henderson in a similar capacity. Reports of these hunters played a significant part in Henderson's decision to acquire lands from the Cherokee Indians in the spring of 1775.

The opening of the transmontane region cast the Long Hunter in a new role. Again, like the mountain men of the Rockies, who later served as guides for immigrant parties bound for Oregon and California, the Long Hunters provided indispensable information to settlers and speculators and piloted hundreds of pioneers to desirable farmlands west of the Appalachians. In general, the Long Hunters had no quarrel with the occupation of the wilderness, for many of them, no less than the immigrants whom they escorted across the mountains, aspired to dwell in the latter-day Canaans which they envisioned.

In many respects John and Samuel Pringle were prototypes of the western immigrant guides. In 1769, almost as soon as the Iroquois and Cherokees had relinquished any part of their claims to lands west of the Alleghenies, the brothers led a party of settlers from the Potomac Valley to lands along the Buckhannon River in northern West Virginia, where during their years as hunters they had found an unusual abundance of rich land, wild fruits and berries, and game animals.

If Kentucky cannot claim the distinction of having the first Long Hunter turned immigrant guide, she nevertheless had in Daniel Boone the most noted one. His enthusiasm undampened by his unfortunate experience at Cumberland Gap, Boone sold his farm upon his return to the Yadkin Valley and moved to the Holston settlements, where a frontier population was poised for another thrust westward. Many of these men and women, long inured to the rigors of a frontier environment, would in 1773, with Boone as their pilot, attempt, unsuccessfully as it turned out, to make a settlement in Bluegrass Kentucky. Two years later, with the backing of Richard Henderson, Boone led a band of settlers to central Kentucky, where they founded a station appropriately named Boonesborough, but by then James Harrod had already claimed the distinction of planting the first settlement in Kentucky.

3

The Advance into Kentucky

THE TREATIES of Hard Labor and Fort Stanwix sig-
naled the end of a golden era for Long Hunters and fur
traders in the trans-Appalachian region and the triumph
of powerful combinations of speculators and of thousands of settlers determined to be the architects of their
own fortunes and to mold the territory to their own interests and desires. An immediate effect of the treaties
was the resuscitation of older speculative organizations,
including the Greenbrier and Loyal companies and the
Ohio Company of Virginia. The Suffering Traders, who,
as the Illinois Company, had earlier sought a grant on
the lower Ohio and Mississippi rivers, also formed the
Indiana Company, thereby giving themselves the option
of later pressing for lands either north or south of the
Ohio River, as might at the time appear wiser. Moreover, beneficiaries of Virginia's military grant, including
George Washington and other officers, who had purchased bounties given to soldiers in the French and Indian War, petitioned the Crown in 1763 for sufficient
lands at the confluence of the Ohio and Mississippi
rivers to satisfy the warrants which they held.

Not surprisingly, a great wave of settlement began to
roll across the Appalachians in the spring of 1769. Three
prongs of the advance led directly to the first penetra-
tions of Kentucky. The first carried hundreds of families

from eastern and central Pennsylvania and the upper Potomac sections of Virginia and Maryland to the region around the Forks of the Ohio and the middle Monongahela Valley. Already scores of pioneers had taken up lands there in defiance of the Proclamation of 1763 and efforts of the government of Pennsylvania and Colonel Henry Bouquet, the commandant at Fort Pitt, to drive them out. When Pennsylvania, brushing aside the claims of Virginia to the region, set up a land office at Pittsburgh in April 1769, the demand for land was so great that 2,790 applicants stormed its doors the day that it was opened. Within a few years Pittsburgh and other settlements on the upper Ohio became important points of departure for surveyors, speculators, and settlers bound for Kentucky.

At the same time other pioneers from the central parts of the Valley of Virginia began to cross the rugged southern portions of the Alleghenies into the Greenbrier region, which had twice during the preceding fifteen years been depopulated by Indian incursions. Attractive lands and energetic action by the Greenbrier Company contributed to a relatively rapid movement into the Greenbrier Valley. These settlements became a springboard for an advance down the Kanawha and Ohio rivers to Kentucky and other parts of the Ohio Valley.

With respect to the earliest occupation of Kentucky, one of the most important advances westward in the wake of the treaties of Hard Labor and Fort Stanwix was into the watershed of the Holston River, particularly along such tributaries as the Watauga, French Broad, and Nolichucky. The Holston country drew thousands of settlers from Virginia, North Carolina, and even Maryland and Pennsylvania and became, in turn, a dispersal center for pioneers bound for Kentucky and Tennessee. It also became a seedbed for frontier leadership and provided essential experiences for a number of men, including James Robertson, John Sevier, and Evan and Isaac Shelby, who would later play significant roles in shaping the course of Kentucky and Tennessee history.

Although Stephen Holston, a hunter, had built a cabin in 1746 on the stream that bears his name, he and a few others who joined him were driven out by hostile Indians. Credit for planting the first enduring settlement on the waters of the Holston, therefore, has traditionally been given to William Bean, a trader and farmer from Pittsylvania County, Virginia. In 1769 Bean erected a cabin at the confluence of Boone's Creek and the Watauga. From there he sent out glowing reports of the fertile lands, plentiful game, and natural beauty of the region. Border residents from southwestern Virginia, many of them Bean's friends and former neighbors, soon arrived, and within two years their clearings extended for several miles along the Watauga.

Meanwhile, settlers were pouring into other parts of the Holston Valley. In 1770 two Virginians, John Carter and William Parker, established a store and trading post near present Rogersville, Tennessee, for the accommodation of travelers bound for Natchez and for carrying on an Indian trade. The year after this settlement in Carter's Valley, Evan Shelby, a Maryland frontiersman and trader, and his son Isaac, later to be the first governor of Kentucky, set up a store at Sapling Grove (present Bristol) and laid the basis for the North-of-Holston settlements. Among the "North Holston" pioneers were Daniel Boone, Valentine Sevier, and the latter's son John. Many of them had been Shelby's neighbors in Maryland. In 1771, also, Jacob Brown purchased the preemption claim of John Ryan on the Nolichucky River and settled a few families, most of them from North Carolina.

Happily for the Watauga settlements, they were visited in the autumn of 1770 by James Robertson, who was to become their most distinguished leader and later to be hailed as the "Father of Tennessee." A native of

39

Brunswick County, Virginia, Robertson was at the time of his visit a resident of Orange County, North Carolina. Following a common frontier practice, he got a corn crop well started and returned to North Carolina for his family. The next spring he and sixteen neighbors settled on the Doe River, a tributary of the Watauga, which in time became the center of the Watauga habitations. Robertson was so burdened by the care of a widowed mother and a host of younger brothers and sisters that he did not learn to read and write until after his marriage at twenty-six years of age. He was nevertheless possessed of exceptional native ability and endowed with superlative qualities of leadership. Inasmuch as he emigrated from a part of North Carolina torn by the Regulator movement, Robertson may have been a Regulator. At the time of the battle of the Alamance, however, he had already moved to the Watauga.

Robertson's relationship to the Regulator movement is but one aspect of a broader question as to whether the migration from the North Carolina backcountry to the Watauga was due largely to the defeat of the Regulators in 1771. There can be no doubt that many of those from the Yadkin Valley were seeking escape from burdensome taxes, excessive quitrents imposed by Lord Granville, inadequate protection from hostile Indians, and the presence of a dangerous criminal element in the backcountry, none of which had excited any sympathy on the part of Governor William Tryon. Since these grievances were essentially those of the Regulators, older historians have contended that a substantial part of the Watauga settlers were Regulators, a view shared by the Tennessee historian Stanley J. Folmsbee. On the other hand, Thomas Perkins Abernethy holds that most Regulators made their peace with the North Carolina authorities after the battle of the Alamance. Abernethy concedes, however, that men of Regulator principles moved into the Holston country in considerable numbers.

Whether large numbers of the Watauga settlers were Regulators is of less significance than the fact that their leaders, regardless of origin, were prone to question governmental policies and given to bold and decisive action. These qualities rose to the surface when the Donelson survey of 1771 disclosed that, contrary to the popular belief that the Holston settlements were in Virginia, all except those north of the Holston were in the Indian territory. Those on the Watauga and Nolichucky rivers and in Carter's Valley had not been included in the cession by the Cherokees. Choosing not to defy both the Indians and John Stuart, the Indian superintendent, John Carter and the residents of Carter's Valley and Jacob Brown and his followers on the Nolichucky abandoned their homes and joined the settlers on the Watauga. With strength derived from their numbers and the compactness of their communities, the three groups decided to stand their ground against any attempt to force them to leave.

Knowing that private purchases of land from the Indians were illegal under the Proclamation of 1763 but convinced that some understanding with the Cherokee claimants was essential, the Wataugans undertook to obtain long-term leases from the Indians. James Robertson and Robert Bean took advantage of cordial relations then existing between the British and the Cherokees to negotiate a ten-year lease of a large tract south and east of the South Fork of the Holston. Shortly afterward Jacob Brown concluded a similar agreement for a tract on the Nolichucky and reestablished the settlements there.

Where the funds for the leases came from remains something of a mystery, but it is not unlikely that some speculator, possibly Judge Richard Henderson of North Carolina, advanced them in the hope that the leases might ultimately become the basis for sales by the Cherokees. If so, it was but an example of the often close relationships between speculators and settlers in the thrust of the frontier westward to Kentucky.

41

Since neither Virginia nor North Carolina recognized their right to reside in the Indian country, the Wataugans took steps to provide themselves with a body of laws and a governing authority. In May 1772 an assembly of arms-bearing men drew up a compact, known as the Watauga Association, by which the government was placed in the hands of a court composed of five members, a sheriff, and a clerk. The original members of the court, which had both legislative and judicial powers, were John Carter, James Robertson, his cousin Charles Robertson, Zachariah Isbell, and Jacob Brown. James Smith, a former Long Hunter, apparently served as the first clerk, with John Sevier and Felix Walker his successors. Holders of the sheriff's office are unknown, but it appears that one of them was Valentine Sevier. The governing authorities were charged with the maintenance of order, the enlistment of a militia for defense, the recording of wills and deeds, the issuance of marriage licenses, and the trial of offenders against the law.

Far from being a great landmark in the history of American democracy, the Watauga Association was, as Ray Billington has pointed out, "an ordinary squatters agreement, stemming from necessity and rooted in Presbyterian religious beliefs which emphasized the original compact between God and man." Its framers regarded it as a temporary expedient designed to serve only until a permanent government should be established and as essential to the protection of the illegal holdings of the Watauga settlers. At peace with the Cherokees and provided with a workable government, the Watauga settlers enjoyed two years of serenity in which they followed the quiet pursuits of clearing their fields, hunting wild game, and rolling back the great forests.

Less fortunate was the small settlement made in Powell Valley in 1769 by Joseph Martin of Albemarle County, Virginia. It owed its beginning to Thomas Walker, who was again vigorously pushing the interests of the Loyal Company and who had sponsored a race between two bands of settlers bent upon occupying lands beyond the Holston. With about twenty men, Martin built cabins, planted corn, and hunted for bear, deer, and buffalo. He remained at the lonely outpost, nearly a hundred miles from the Holston settlements, until hostile Indians forced him to leave. With the restoration of peace in 1774 he returned, and Martin's Station became an important stopping place for pioneers bound for Kentucky.

While the Watauga settlers were schooling themselves in frontier experiences which would prove useful when they crossed the mountains into Bluegrass Kentucky and central Tennessee, the Indiana Company was engaged in political activity that would have made much of the trans-Appalachian region into a fourteenth colony. Confirmation of the grant made to it by the Treaty of Fort Stanwix at first appeared remote, since Lord Hillsborough, an implacable enemy of the scheme, had on March 12, 1768, been named to the cabinet post of Secretary of State for the American Department. Nevertheless, the company in early 1769 sent Samuel Wharton to London to press its claims. Wharton assiduously cultivated the friendship of powerful politicians and proved so adept at political maneuver that he alienated Hillsborough from most of the other members of the cabinet.

During the summer of 1769 Wharton scored another coup by enlarging the company to include some of the most influential administrative and Parliamentary officials in England. Among them was the wealthy and powerful London merchant Thomas Walpole. Thereafter the organization, now officially styled the Grand Ohio Company, was popularly referred to as the Walpole Company in recognition of its most aggressive English promoter. The enlarged syndicate proposed to purchase 2.4 million acres of land for which it would offer the Crown £10,460, or the exact amount the British gov-

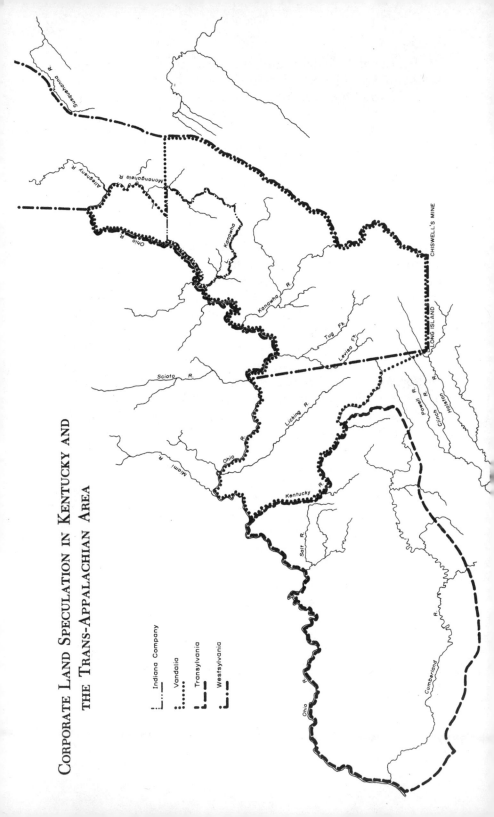

CORPORATE LAND SPECULATION IN KENTUCKY AND
THE TRANS-APPALACHIAN AREA

Indiana Company
Vandalia
Transylvania
Westsylvania

ernment had paid the Iroquois for the cession at Fort Stanwix. The plan obviated the necessity of a separate petition by the old Indiana Company and had the additional advantage of enjoying broad political support.

Expecting an unalterable and perhaps decisive opposition by Lord Hillsborough, the members of the company were astonished when Hillsborough made a counterproposal that it enlarge its request to 20 million acres, or a tract sufficient to establish a separate colony. The secretary's motives are yet obscure, but he apparently expected that the price for such a vast tract would be about £100,000, a sum beyond the reach of the petitioners. Nevertheless, the plans of the Grand Ohio Company moved closer to realization when on January 14, 1770, Wharton and Walpole came to an understanding with the Treasury Commissioners that the price would remain at £10,460.

Other impediments in the path of the company also proved less obstructive than anticipated. Edward Montague, the agent of the Virginia House of Burgesses in London, entered a caveat against the petition, which delayed action but did not seriously endanger the company's request. Moreover, William Nelson, who became acting governor of Virginia upon the death of Lord Botetourt, took the position that most of the grants made by Virginia had lapsed because of failure of the grantees to comply with their terms and professed satisfaction with the promise of the Grand Ohio Company to respect all legitimate prior rights to lands lying within the proposed colony. Nor did the Loyal Company raise serious objections, since it had apparently already reached an understanding with the Suffering Traders at the Treaty of Fort Stanwix and since most of its lands lay outside the tract requested by the Grand Ohio Company. Finally, the company agreed to provide lands to satisfy the military grant promised the Virginia Regiment by Governor Robert Dinwiddie in 1754.

Although opposition to the proposals of the Grand

Ohio Company appeared to be diminishing, the British governmental machinery moved with customary slowness. Not until July 1, 1772, did the Committee on Plantation Affairs act favorably on the company's petition. By then Lord Hillsborough had once more become the open enemy of the scheme. His influence in the cabinet, however, which had been waning for nearly three years, was fast approaching its nadir, and on August 14, 1772, he was forced to resign. On the same day the Privy Council gave its approval to the petition of the company.

Lying within the proposed colony, to be named Vandalia in honor of Queen Caroline of England, who claimed descent from the Vandals, was the eastern third of Kentucky. The boundaries of Vandalia, as defined on May 6, 1773, embraced a considerably larger area than the Grand Ohio Company had originally sought. Included were most of southwestern Pennsylvania between the Monongahela and Ohio rivers, the part of West Virginia west of the Fairfax estate and the Greenbrier River, and all of Kentucky east of a boundary drawn from the mouth of the Kentucky River to its source and thence to the intersection of the Holston River and the Virginia–North Carolina border. The part of Kentucky lying between the Kentucky River and a line drawn from Cumberland Gap to the mouth of the Scioto had not been part of the original request of the Grand Ohio Company, but it was included as a result of the survey of the Donelson Line.

Despite the favorable auguries of the late summer of 1772, dark days lay ahead for Vandalia. On July 14, 1773, the Crown Law Officers submitted a report critical of the vagueness of the boundaries proposed and of plans for the collection of quitrents. Of even greater importance, the Boston Tea Party of December 16, 1773, and the resultant actions by the British Parliament heightened an atmosphere of crisis which had prevailed in relations between England and her American colo-

46

nies for several years. For these reasons George III declined to place the royal seal upon the Vandalia grant.

As the prospects for Vandalia dimmed, Virginia experienced a burst of expansionist activity between 1772 and 1775 seldom matched in her history. Speculators, including organized groups, who had been relatively quiescent during the years when settlement west of the Alleghenies had been forbidden and who had been forced to adapt their own designs to the rising fortunes of the Grand Ohio Company, now sprang to life. In their activities they found a staunch ally in John Murray, the Earl of Dunmore, who arrived in Williamsburg on December 12, 1771, as the new governor of Virginia.

Dunmore gave tangible encouragement to Virginia speculators by creating new political jurisdictions for the territory west of the Alleghenies and south of the Ohio. In 1772 all of Kentucky and the parts of Virginia and West Virginia south of the New and Kanawha rivers were included in the new county of Fincastle, which was carved from Botetourt. The following year, in a move to counteract Pennsylvania's assertions of authority over the region around the Forks of the Ohio, Dunmore carefully delineated the boundaries of the hitherto somewhat amorphous District of West Augusta and provided it with its own governing officials.

The formation of Fincastle County clearly presaged an advance into Kentucky. As in other new administrative jurisdictions, officials of Fincastle County were drawn largely from men with strong speculative interests. The most influential member of its government was William Preston, a prominent landholder and a nephew of James Patton, who had been one of the most powerful land barons in the Valley of Virginia. Other officials included William Christian, John Floyd, Arthur Campbell, William Russell, and Evan Shelby, all of whom would play conspicuous parts in early Kentucky history. The authority of the new county also promised added validity to surveys based upon military warrants, which the governor had decided to issue in accordance with the Proclamation of 1763.

Dunmore's benevolent attitude toward the speculators was, as most knowledgeable Virginians perceived, almost certainly behind a titillating announcement by Thomas Bullitt in Virginia and Pennsylvania newspapers in December 1772. Bullitt, a native of Fauquier County, Virginia, stated that he planned to go to Kentucky in the spring of 1773 to lay out surveys based upon military warrants and invited others interested in military surveys to join him with chain carriers and "other necessaries." Without Dunmore's approval, Bullitt could hardly have offered to register surveys and obtain grants for holders of military certificates.

Further evidence that Bullitt was closely linked to Dunmore stems from his appointment by John Connolly, soon to be the governor's agent at Fort Pitt, rather than by William Preston, the surveyor of Fincastle County. Bullitt's plans, however, extended beyond the laying out of military grants, and his agreement to survey lands containing salt springs and lead mines for George Morgan, an associate of Samuel Wharton, suggests a possible alliance with the Grand Ohio Company.

Although Bullitt had advertised that he expected to be at the mouth of the Scioto River by April 15, the spring of 1773 was well advanced when he set out down the Ohio. He did not arrive at Pittsburgh until April 20, and it was not until May 11 that he and thirty-odd white men and three Indians, with their supplies, embarked upon the Ohio aboard a batteau and three canoes. Among the members of Bullitt's party were James Harrod and Hancock Taylor, a surveyor. A number of Virginia officers had entrusted their surveys to Taylor, who in 1769 had led a party of Long Hunters to Kentucky. Harrod, who in 1767 had visited Kentucky and Tennessee, probably served as a guide for Bullitt's expedition.

The journey down the upper Ohio was uneventful, and on May 29 the surveyors reached the mouth of the Kanawha River. There they were joined by James, Robert, and George McAfee, Samuel Adams, and James McCoun of Botetourt County, who had descended the Kanawha. Following them down the Ohio was yet a third party of seven members, led by twenty-year-old Isaac Hite, a grandson of Joist Hite, the prominent Valley of Virginia speculator. Hite and his men later joined the other surveyors in Kentucky.

The Kentucky-bound surveyors and land-seekers were well aware of the claims of the Shawnee Indians to territory south of the Ohio River and of the cavalier disregard for their rights in the Treaty of Fort Stanwix. Hoping to prevent any hostile actions against the surveyors, Bullitt and six companions, including the three Indians with the expedition, left the main party for the Shawnee village of Chillicothe. Uninformed of the impending visit by any advance runner, as was the custom, the Indians, somewhat bewildered by Bullitt's unannounced arrival, locked him and his companions up for the night, while they pondered a course of action.

The next day about a hundred warriors, painted and brandishing tomahawks, appeared before the place where the members of the surveying parties were confined and escorted them to the tribal council house. Instead of being scalped, as he had expected, Bullitt was ordered to make a speech. In his address, more noted for its effect than for its honesty, Bullitt assured the Shawnees that Governor Dunmore would soon visit them and pay them for their lands south of the Ohio and promised them that, as "brothers," they could continue to hunt there. The Shawnees, for their part, agreed not to molest the surveyors in their work. Bullitt's misrepresentations thus gained valuable time needed for making the surveys, but they also contributed to a rapid deterioration in relations with the western tribes that led to Dunmore's War less than eighteen months later.

After an absence of five days, Bullitt and his party rejoined the main body of surveyors, and together they continued down the Ohio. On June 17 they arrived at Salt Lick Run, or present Vanceburg, Kentucky, the site of an important salt pond, frequented by deer and buffalo and visited by Indians for countless generations. There Bullitt projected the first of several towns which he planned to establish at regular intervals along the Ohio. The naming of numerous streams, including Bracken, Taylor, Woolper, Kennedy, Lee, and Tygart creeks, served as a useful record of the parts of Kentucky visited by the surveyors at the time.

Enlarged on June 29 by the arrival of Isaac Hite and his six companions, Bullitt's company continued on to the Big Bone Lick. There it found mastodon tusks over eleven feet long, and James Douglas made use of giant ribs for tent poles. Bullitt selected the Big Bone Lick as the site for another of his towns. From there smaller parties began to range into the surrounding country in search of good land and salt springs.

On July 7 the McAfee brothers, James McCoun, and Samuel Adams, accompanied by Hancock Taylor and two of his assistants, left the base at Big Bone Lick and for nearly four weeks selected and surveyed tracts in central Kentucky, apparently in the hope of acquiring them under legal provisions for settlement rights. During their explorations they followed the Kentucky River to the salt lick at Drennon's Creek, made surveys near Frankfort in the vicinity of the first Kentucky state capitol, and examined much of the region between present Lawrenceburg and Harrodsburg. By July 31 they had laid off twenty-three separate tracts, mostly in the canelands on Salt River, and in some cases had made small improvements in the form of crude cabins, lean-tos, or simple brush clearings.

On July 31 McAfee's men left Taylor near Harrodsburg and started homeward. Traveling by way of the Kentucky River, they crossed the Pine and Cumberland mountains and on August 15 reached the settlements on the Clinch River. There they visited William Russell at "Castlewood," where they found Russell laying plans to lead an immigrant party to Kentucky, with Daniel Boone as its guide.

Meanwhile, Bullitt continued down the Ohio. At the mouth of the Kentucky he encountered a large party of Delaware hunters, and at the Falls of the Ohio he and his men were visited by a band of Kickapoos, but neither proved hostile. Bullitt established a base camp at the site of Louisville, where he surveyed tracts for John Connolly and Charles Warnsdorf. Rights of the latter were later transferred to Connolly and John Campbell jointly. Contiguous tracts were laid off for Edward Ward, the half-brother of George Croghan, and for friends of the Pennsylvania trader. Grants based upon these surveys were important to the alliance which Lord Dunmore was then forging with powerful leaders in the Pittsburgh region and which, it was hoped, would add strength to Virginia's claim to territory at the Forks of the Ohio.

Bullitt, as well as James Douglas, Isaac Hite, John Mann, Ebenezer Severns, and others, also marked off lands west of the Falls and along Salt River. Their location beyond the Donelson Line violated agreements with the Cherokees but had no special relevance to the Shawnees, who had not surrendered their claims to any part of Kentucky.

It is possible only to speculate about the activities of James Harrod at this time. There is reason to believe that he accompanied Bullitt to the Falls of the Ohio and that he left the party to make explorations of his own, possibly on the basis of reports of Hancock Taylor, who appears to have rejoined Bullitt after the departure of the McAfees. Presumably Harrod went southeastward by way of Benson Creek, Knob Lick, and the Kentucky River and in the summer of 1773 visited the site of Harrodsburg. Lending credence to this supposition is the near-certainty that Harrod was not with the McAfees and Hancock Taylor in July 1773 and doubt that he would have chosen Harrodsburg as the location of his settlement in 1774 had he not previously been there.

September found the surveying parties returning homeward. They had learned much concerning central Kentucky, but apparently they had not made use of the buffalo trail leading from the mouth of Limestone Creek, or present Maysville, to the Bluegrass region. Instead, they had followed the Kentucky River into the interior, even though the route was about 150 miles longer. They had also failed to join forces with a party of Pennsylvania surveyors, under Captain William Thompson, who were establishing claims along the Licking River.

Quite apart from its adventurous character and the intriguing questions it raises about the activities of the surveyors, Bullitt's expedition is of interest for the light that it sheds upon the political atmosphere in which the first surveys were made in Kentucky. When Bullitt sought to register the tracts delineated in the summer of 1773, William Preston, the surveyor of Fincastle County, refused to enter the plats on the ground that, contrary to law, no deputy surveyor of that county had been present when the surveys were made and that the tracts were west of the Donelson Line. Moreover, even while Bullitt's party was yet in Kentucky, Sir William Johnson complained to Lord Dartmouth, the Secretary of State for the American Department, that the surveyors had gone beyond the boundaries of the proposed colony of Vandalia and laid off lands which they intended to patent. Dunmore denied that he had authorized Bullitt and others to survey lands west of the Donelson Line, but he lost little time in issuing patents to tracts at the Falls of the Ohio to John Connolly and Charles Warnsdorf on the basis of surveys made by Bullitt and directed Preston to record them in the Fincastle County plat book.

A proclamation by Dunmore on December 15, 1773, inspired perhaps in part by the waning fortunes of the Grand Ohio Company, enabled holders of military warrants to locate tracts wherever they might choose and paved the way for a new invasion of the trans-Allegheny country by ambitious speculators. In the spring of 1774 William Preston dispatched a surveying party to Kentucky under the direction of his deputy, John Floyd. Hancock Taylor, James Douglas, and Isaac Hite, three experienced surveyors who had accompanied Bullitt to Kentucky the previous year, were in Floyd's company.

Floyd and his associates left Preston's residence in Fincastle County on April 7, preceded by a few days by an advance party under Taylor. Proceeding by way of the New and Kanawha rivers, they met John Field, of Culpeper County, who was then making surveys in the Kanawha Valley above Charleston. Although Field informed them that the Shawnees had become distinctly hostile, Floyd and his men continued on to the mouth of the Kanawha. There they found twenty-six men encamped, some with intentions of cultivating the land and others awaiting Floyd's arrival before going on to Kentucky. On April 22 the surveyors loaded their supplies aboard four canoes and left the Kanawha for Kentucky.

Warnings of Shawnee unrest were confirmed on April 26, when three men arrived at Floyd's camp with a harrowing tale of their capture by the Indians, who had taken all their belongings and then set them free. Floyd also received reports of an attack at Beaver Creek on April 15 in which one man lost his life and another was wounded. In addition, there were disconcerting rumors that George Croghan, who sought to preserve his trading interests in spite of his desire for land, had urged the Indians to kill the Virginians and rob the Pennsylvanians who ventured into their territory.

Although four of his men decided to return home, Floyd and thirty-two companions continued on down the Ohio, passing many sites previously visited by Bullitt and his associates. En route they laid off tracts for several prominent Virginians, including one for Patrick Henry at the old Shawnee village opposite the mouth of the Scioto River, another at the Big Bone Lick for William Christian, despite a prior claim by Thomas Bullitt, and another four miles above the mouth of the Miami for Hugh Mercer.

On May 14 the company reached the mouth of the Kentucky, where it encamped for nine days awaiting an emissary of William Preston, who was expected to provide definitive information concerning the location of the Donelson Line. Eleven of the men, perhaps led by David Williams, went up the Kentucky for about a hundred miles, where, as they knew, James Harrod was already "building a kind of Town." When no messenger from Preston came, the remainder of the surveyors resumed their journey down the Ohio.

The Shawnees, who had offered little resistance to the occupation of the western slopes of the Alleghenies, now stiffened their resolve to retain their Kentucky hunting grounds. Through bitter experience they had learned that the coming of surveyors meant that settlers were not far behind. Three days after leaving the mouth of the Kentucky, Floyd's party encountered two Indians, who stated that war between the tribes and the Virginians seemed likely and that they were out to call in their hunters. They told Floyd that already one skirmish on the upper Ohio had cost the lives of sixteen Indians. The apparent imminence of war led a few of Floyd's men to favor going on to New Orleans, but other counsels prevailed, and the surveyors decided to lay off lands until they were driven out of Kentucky by superior force.

On May 29 Floyd and Taylor reached the Falls of the Ohio, where the remainder of their company gathered the following day. Unrestrained by any clarification of the Donelson Line, they, like their predecessors of the previous summer, continued to mark off tracts beyond the Kentucky River. At the Falls of the Ohio Douglas resurveyed lands already granted to John Connolly and Charles Warnsdorf. On May 31 the men divided into two parties, one under Taylor and the other under Floyd. Taylor's men generally moved northeastward along the Ohio and on the waters of Harrod's Creek, while Floyd swung to the south and along the branches of Beargrass Creek. Surveys were made for numerous Virginians, including William Byrd, Alexander Spotswood, Hugh Mercer, William Christian, and William Fleming. After the two parties reunited near the headwaters of Sinking Fork of Beargrass Creek, Taylor set out for the Kentucky River and parts of central Kentucky with which he had become familiar the preceding year. It is not unlikely that he visited Harrodsburg, which was then beginning to take shape as a settlement.

Floyd, meanwhile, was having his troubles. Lands on Salt River, where he made surveys, were generally uninviting. Worse yet, James Knox, an experienced Long Hunter who apparently served as his guide, deserted and left for Harrodsburg. Forced to curtail all activities for several days because of illness, Floyd decided to leave for the Kentucky River to search for Taylor. At one time he was very near Taylor's men, who made surveys on the site of Frankfort and on the South Fork of Elkhorn Creek. Not until July 1 did the two companies meet again.

After setting up a common base at Taylor's camp on the South Fork of Elkhorn Creek, the surveyors resumed their work. Floyd and William Nash scouted the country along the North Fork of the Elkhorn, during which they discovered "Floyd's Spring" near Georgetown. A few days later the surveyors divided into three groups, led by Floyd, Taylor, and William Douglas. During the following weeks Douglas made extensive surveys in present Jessamine County, Floyd located tracts on the Dix River, and Taylor worked in other

55

parts of central Kentucky. At the end of July Taylor and two companions were attacked by Indians while paddling down the Kentucky River. One of the men, James Strother, was killed instantly, and Taylor himself received wounds which led to his death two days later.

With tension on the frontiers steadily mounting, William Preston asked William Russell to warn the surveyors in Kentucky of their danger. For the mission Russell chose Daniel Boone and Michael Stoner, both experienced Kentucky Long Hunters. Russell instructed Boone and Stoner to follow the Kentucky River to the Ohio, proceed downstream to the Falls, and then return by way of the Cumberland, under the assumption that somewhere en route they would find the surveyors at work.

The surveying parties, well aware of their perilous situation, had already begun to leave Kentucky. On August 9 Floyd's company arrived at Blackburn's Station at Rye Cove, on the Clinch River, and from there went on to William Preston's residence at Smithfield, or Draper's Meadows, on New River. Taylor's men reached "Castlewood," the home of William Russell, on the same day that Boone and Stoner returned from Kentucky. Their simultaneous arrival lends credence to Boone's claim that he "conducted in the surveyors," but it seems likely that when he and Stoner encountered them, they were already on their way home.

Whatever hopes of success Thomas Bullitt had in 1773 of winning a reprieve from any hostile actions by the Shawnees proved by the end of the summer of 1774 to have been illusory. For the Indians, too much was at stake to permit an unchallenged advance by surveyors and settlers into Kentucky. The danger that was apprehended by the surveyors, who wisely left Kentucky, was by then evident throughout the entire transmontane country. Before the leaves had fallen in the autumn of 1774, the war which all had dreaded would be at hand.

4

A Year of Crisis

For THE SHAWNEES and other tribes northwest of the Ohio River the year 1773 had a more ominous cast than had any since 1763, when the British won undisputed control of the Ohio Valley. The ever-increasing numbers of Long Hunters in Kentucky and other areas south of the Ohio in the 1760s had by then raised the specter of a land depleted of game and the probability of real want among the tribes. Worse still, in the wake of the treaties of Hard Labor and Fort Stanwix, both of which had ignored the claims of the Shawnees to parts of the Ohio Valley, the spring of 1769 had released a flood of immigrants into the trans-Allegheny country. By 1773 the flood was approaching tidal proportions around the Forks of the Ohio, and lesser waves were lapping at lowlands as far south as the Kanawha. At the southern end of the Valley of Virginia yet another pressure was building on the waters of the Holston, which could lead only to expansion into Kentucky and Tennessee. When Thomas Bullitt and his large company of surveyors appeared in Kentucky in the summer of 1773, the Indians knew that settlers would soon follow and that they faced one of the gravest moments in their history.

Nor could the Shawnees take comfort in the thought that violations of their territory were the work of a few impatient and avaricious men, for all too soon they found that Governor Dunmore had approved and encouraged the first advances into Kentucky. At the very time that Bullitt's party was making surveys in Kentucky, Dunmore was visiting Fort Pitt and laying plans for a vigorous assertion of Virginia authority over that strategic area. Already, in 1769, Pennsylvania had opened a land office in the disputed region and provided it with a government, first as part of Westmoreland County and a year later separately as Bedford County. When about six hundred irate Virginians who had settled there, led by the popular and impetuous Michael Cresap, petitioned the Virginia authorities to provide them with a government, Dunmore undertook a personal inspection of the situation. His journey to Fort Pitt convinced him—if he needed convincing—that Virginia should immediately extend her authority over the region. To that end the council of the colony on October 11, 1773, created the District of West Augusta, which included not only the area in dispute with Pennsylvania but also most of trans-Allegheny West Virginia.

Of more immediate importance to the future of Kentucky were agreements which Dunmore reached with George Croghan and John Connolly at Fort Pitt. Croghan was rankling under the refusal of Pennsylvania to recognize the grant of 200,000 acres near the Forks of the Ohio made to him in 1747 by the Iroquois and confirmed by them in the treaty of Fort Stanwix. When the Vandalia scheme, on which he then pinned his hopes, collapsed, he was left with no alternative except to reach some accord with Virginia. In acknowledging Croghan's rights, Dunmore gained an ally whose influence with the Indians was unsurpassed and who might prove invaluable to his future plans.

The alliance with Croghan was unfortunately partially negated by Dunmore's naming of Connolly, the nephew of Croghan, as his agent at Fort Pitt, now renamed Fort Dunmore. Connolly had neither the desire nor the wisdom to cultivate friendly relations with the Indians, and in placing him in a position of considerable authority, Dunmore could hardly have done more to foster fear and insecurity among frontier residents and to inflame the hostility of the Indians.

The relatively unmolested activities of surveyors in central Kentucky and along the Kanawha and Big Sandy rivers in the summer of 1773, as well as the governor's arrangements at Fort Pitt, must have offered encouragement to Daniel Boone and his family, who in September left the Yadkin Valley for Kentucky. The Boones traveled by way of Wolf Hills, or Abingdon, Virginia, to William Russell's residence on the Clinch River. There they were joined by the Russells and several other families. The enlarged party included about thirty men, among whom were Squire Boone, Michael Stoner, David Gass, Isaac Crabtree, William Bush, James and Richard Mendenhall, Edmund Jennings, and Thomas Sharp. In associating himself with Russell, who held the military warrants which were expected to give validity to their land titles, Boone again exemplified the close connection that often existed between the Long Hunters and land speculators.

The prospective immigrants left "Castlewood" in three detachments. The first, led by Boone, included the women and children and essential baggage. Behind it was a party transporting provisions such as flour, farm tools, and other articles. In it were Crabtree, the Mendenhalls, a man named Drake, Henry Russell and James Boone, the latter the sons of Russell and Boone, and two Negro slaves, Charles and Adam. The third contingent, with Russell and Gass in charge, expected to depart somewhat later and to overtake the advance parties in time to travel with them through Cumberland Gap and into central Kentucky.

Tragedy, however, lay in wait for the would-be settlers. On the night of October 9 the company with the provisions, which was about three miles behind the advance party, made camp at Wallen's Creek Ford. About dawn the next morning a band of Shawnees attacked, killing the Mendenhalls and Drake instantly. Henry Russell and James Boone were both shot through the hips and then tortured to death. Charles, who was captured, was claimed by at least two Indians, who settled their dispute by splitting him up with a tomahawk. Only Crabtree and Adam escaped, the latter by concealing himself behind a woodpile, where he witnessed the horrors of the attack.

When Boone learned of the bloody events at Wallen's Creek Ford, he immediately prepared the advance party for an attack, but none came. Later the mutilated bodies of the Boone and Russell youths were found and buried in a common grave. Their sad experience barely fifty miles from Russell's home chilled any enthusiasm for continuing on to Kentucky, and the saddened pioneers turned back. Left homeless, the Boone family settled for the time on property belonging to David Gass.

Although the shadows of an Indian war were already lengthening over the trans-Allegheny region, surveying parties, such as that led by John Floyd into central Kentucky, and large numbers of immigrants resumed the movement across the mountains in the spring of 1774. George Washington promised passage money to America, suspension of quitrents for a period of years, and religious freedom to English, Irish, Scottish, and German immigrants who would settle on his 19,990-acre tract on the Kanawha River, a few miles above its confluence with the Ohio. In March 1774 Washington sent more than twenty "hirelings and servants" from Mount Vernon to prepare the land for settlement, but when they reached Redstone, on the Monongahela, they learned of imminent danger of Indian attacks and decided against continuing with their plan.

More willing to take the risks attendant to frontier advance was James Harrod, who in 1774 founded the first settlement in Kentucky at Harrodsburg. Having already visited Kentucky twice, first in 1767 and again in 1773 as a member of Thomas Bullitt's surveying party, the thirty-two-year-old resident of Ten Mile Creek, in Washington County, Pennsylvania, announced that in the spring of 1774 he would return to Kentucky and invited those who wished to make settlements there to join him. Despite the threatening atmosphere then prevailing in the Ohio Valley, thirty-one young men gathered at the mouth of Grave Creek (present Moundsville, West Virginia), the appointed place of rendezvous.

After holding an election in which the tall, erect, black-bearded Harrod was chosen captain, the party loaded its supplies into dugouts and departed. At the mouth of the Kanawha it met another band of white men en route home and was told in no uncertain terms that Kentucky was no place for settlement. Taking care to avoid roving bands of Indians, Harrod and his men, nevertheless, continued to the mouth of the Kentucky River. They ascended that stream for about a hundred miles and then from a point later known as Harrod's Landing followed an old buffalo trail for about fifteen miles to a site near Salt River, which Harrod selected as the location for his settlement.

The site chosen for the town of Harrodsburg lay in the midst of rich canelands interspersed with open spaces. The lush grasses, clover, and wild rye which covered the ground concealed the gentle slopes and numerous ravines and made the country appear nearly level. The town itself was situated on an eminence and embraced a clear, gushing spring and fine meadowlands. Voicing the approval of those who had accompanied Harrod, one member of the party declared the land "delightful beyond conception."

Harrodstown, as the village was first called, was laid out into thirty-one half-acre in-lots, all fronting upon a main street, which ran in an east-west direction. The plots were numbered and assigned to the men by drawing lots. By similar arrangement each member of the party was provided a ten-acre out-lot for cultivation of crops.

By June 10 the number of men in Harrod's company had increased to forty-two, augmented by eleven who had descended the Ohio with the surveying party under John Floyd. By that time several cabins were already under construction. Following the arrival of Floyd, Harrod divided the men into groups of eight or ten each. Almost immediately the smaller parties began the erection of cabins at several other places along the Salt River, including Harrod's Run, or Mock's Run, Clark's Run, and on the Hanging Fork of Dix River. In doing so the men undoubtedly hoped to establish indisputable claims to substantial amounts of land in central Kentucky.

Settlement of the Bluegrass area, nevertheless, proved premature. On July 8 nine of Harrod's men were making surveys at Fountain Blue Spring, a few miles from Harrodsburg, when they were attacked by a band of twenty Shawnee warriors. James Cowan and James Hamilton were killed. The others escaped and reported the attack to Harrod, who on the following day set out with thirty-five men for the scene of the battle. No sign of the Indians, however, was to be found.

Since they had not yet built a fort and were without adequate means of protection, Harrod and his men decided that they must leave Kentucky. Missing from the company was Jacob Lewis, who had set out on a hunting trip twenty-two days previously and who was presumed dead or captured by the Indians. The pioneers left Harrodsburg on July 9 and reached the Powell Valley settlements on July 29. Clearly, the occupation of Kentucky must await more propitious times.

The attack upon Harrod's men was but one manifestation of a determination already reached by the Shawnees to destroy the spearheads of settlement west of the Allegheny Mountains. In April, only a few weeks after

Harrod had left Grave Creek, a band of Indians at the mouth of the Kanawha River fired upon advance members of a surveying party bound for Kentucky. Overwhelmed with anger, the surveyors, among whom was George Rogers Clark, chose Michael Cresap as their leader and tried to prevail upon him to attack the Indian villages at once. With uncharacteristic restraint, Cresap persuaded them to return to Wheeling, where they might first obtain information regarding any action that Virginia might plan to take against the Indians.

The dissemination of an incendiary circular by John Connolly on April 21 vastly increased the danger to surveying parties in Kentucky and to settlers who had taken up lands west of the mountains. Connolly declared that a virtual state of war already existed in the Ohio Valley and urged all persons exposed to attack to prepare for any emergency. Cresap and a number of aggressive companions needed no further incentive, and during the succeeding weeks engaged in a series of attacks upon the Indians in what was commonly known on the frontier as "Cresap's War."

One of the incidents erroneously attributed to Cresap was the killing of several members of the family of Logan, a friendly Mingo chief, at the mouth of Yellow Creek on April 30. Contemporary accounts of the episode are so contradictory that it is nearly impossible to establish the facts, but it involved the killing of two Mingoes on the north side of the Ohio on April 29 and the premeditated murder of eight other unsuspecting Indians by Daniel Greathouse and other unscrupulous frontiersmen. Thereupon Logan turned into an implacable foe of the white men, and during the following weeks he personally took thirteen scalps. Most of the Indian depredations of the spring and summer of 1774 were apparently the work of Logan and roving parties of Shawnees.

Rash and irresponsible actions by John Connolly, among which was the killing of one of the Indians whom Cornstalk had provided as an escort for traders returning to Fort Dunmore, threatened to precipitate a full-scale Indian war, which could have had only disastrous consequences for surveyors and settlers in Kentucky. Fortunately, George Croghan used his great influence with Kiasutha of the Senecas and Grey Eyes and The Pipe of the Delawares to prevent a general uprising of tribes north of the Ohio.

Meanwhile, Dunmore took steps to set up a defense perimeter extending from Fort Dunmore southward to the mouth of the Kanawha. In June Major William Crawford began construction of Fort Fincastle at Wheeling, and on July 12 Andrew Lewis was ordered to the mouth of the Kanawha, where he later erected a small defense post. Dunmore's decision made no provision for the protection of surveyors and settlers in Kentucky and rendered their situation extremely precarious. Their security depended partly upon a successful outcome of an expedition of some four hundred men which Colonel Angus McDonald led into the Indian country on July 26. Although McDonald advanced from Fort Fincastle without mishap until he was within six miles of his destination, he then suffered a dual setback. An ambush demoralized his army, which arrived at the Indian villages only to find them deserted.

Already, however, Dunmore had laid plans for a far more effective strike against the Indians. On July 24 he informed Andrew Lewis that he himself was proceeding to Fort Dunmore to strengthen defenses on the upper Ohio and to prepare a blow that would break the power of the Indians. He proposed to gather a force of more than a thousand men from the upper Potomac region and the Monongahela Valley and then move down the Ohio from Fort Dunmore. He instructed Lewis to enlist militia from Augusta, Botetourt, and Fincastle counties and to march westward by way of the Kanawha. The two armies would then unite on the Ohio and move into the Indian country as a single force.

64

Speculators and settlers who had long dreamed of the opening of Kentucky responded to news of Dunmore's anticipated expedition with unbounded enthusiasm. The Holston and Clinch valleys, whence so many of Kentucky's pioneers would emigrate, and areas feeding their stream of population to Kentucky by way of the Kanawha Valley were generously represented among both officers and men at Point Pleasant, the only battle of Dunmore's War. Prominent among them were Evan and Isaac Shelby, William Russell, William Fleming, William Preston, William Christian, Henry Pauling, and Samuel McDowell, to mention but a few. Isaac Shelby would later become the first governor of Kentucky, Fleming and Pauling would represent Kentucky counties in the Virginia Constitutional Convention of 1788, and McDowell would serve as president of seven conventions agitating for Kentucky statehood and as president of the state's first constitutional convention in 1792.

Perhaps none of those destined to play important roles in Kentucky history had more reason to take up arms against the Shawnees than James Harrod, whose settlement at Harrodsburg had been broken up a few months earlier by hostile Indians. In the summer of 1773 Harrod had been among those who accompanied William Bullitt on the latter's surveying expedition to Kentucky. The following spring he descended the Ohio with thirty-one men to found the first settlement in Kentucky. Forced to abandon their improvements in July 1774, Harrod and his men set out for Powell Valley, where they learned of Dunmore's planned expedition against the Shawnees. Harrod and twenty-two men who had accompanied him to Kentucky enlisted in the brigade commanded by Colonel William Christian, which was among the troops arriving at Point Pleasant after the battle was over.

The wing of Dunmore's army commanded by Lewis held its rendezvous at Camp Union, or present Lewisburg, West Virginia. An advance force of about six hundred men under Lewis's popular younger brother, Charles, left Camp Union on September 6. Six days later Lewis and Colonel William Fleming departed with another five hundred men. An additional two hundred militia under Christian were to leave on September 25 or 26 and join Lewis at the mouth of the Kanawha.

Upon arriving at Point Pleasant, at the junction of the Kanawha and the Ohio, Lewis found awaiting him a message from Dunmore ordering him to join the governor about twenty-five miles from Chillicothe. Although his men deeply resented a plan which would leave the mouth of the Kanawha undefended, Lewis prepared to obey Dunmore's instructions.

Before he could break camp, Lewis was attacked by some eight hundred to eleven hundred Indian warriors led by Cornstalk. The Indians had observed the movements of both Dunmore and Lewis and had correctly surmised the strategy planned by the governor. For Cornstalk, any hope of success against such overwhelming odds lay in striking the two armies before they could unite and defeating them separately. Accordingly, on the night of October 9 his braves crossed the Ohio to the south, or West Virginia, side. At dawn the Indians fired upon Valentine Sevier and James Robinson, who had left Lewis's camp to hunt for turkeys. The two hunters, along with others who had gone out, hastened back to camp with reports that Indians were lurking about.

Lewis immediately ordered his brother Charles and William Fleming, each with about 150 men, to scout the areas along the Ohio and Kanawha rivers. About sunrise the Indians unleashed a full-scale attack. Their army, made up chiefly of Shawnees, Delawares, Mingoes, and Ottawas, concentrated its force against the detachment led by Charles Lewis and mortally wounded the young officer. Belatedly recognizing the magnitude of the Indian assault, Andrew Lewis sent out another force.

66

under Colonel John Field, who also received fatal wounds. By that time Fleming's men had been routed, and Fleming himself had sustained severe, but not mortal, wounds.

From dawn until dusk the battle raged. Displaying superb generalship, Cornstalk, known for his fine voice and convincing speech, constantly urged his warriors to give evidence of their valor and to destroy the enemy. Sheer courage and willingness to fight for their homes and hunting lands, however, could not prevail against superior numbers, and the arrival of more troops from Botetourt and Augusta counties could weight the balance heavily against the Indians. Still Lewis was unable to deliver a decisive blow. When Isaac Shelby led a flanking movement along the east bank of Crooked Creek, a small tributary of the Kanawha, Cornstalk mistakenly assumed that further reinforcements for Lewis were arriving. Believing that it would be foolish to continue the battle under such unfavorable conditions, the Shawnee chief decided to give up. As night came on the Indians gathered the bodies of their fallen from the field of battle and placed them in the Ohio River, after which they retired to the north bank of that stream. Their losses have never been ascertained, but they were probably comparable to those of Lewis, whose casualties numbered forty-six men killed and eighty wounded.

The significance of the battle of Point Pleasant was immediately apparent to both the Indians and the Virginians. Convinced that the tribes could not muster enough strength to withstand the full force of Dunmore's offensive, Cornstalk returned to his people and offered them a choice bitter in the extreme. Rising to the dramatic heights of which he was capable, he proposed that they kill their women and children and that the men then continue their fight until not one was left. The only other alternative was to sue for peace. With heavy hearts the Shawnees and their allies resigned themselves to surrender. Once they had made their decision, Cornstalk dispatched Matthew Elliott, a white man, to seek a conference with Lord Dunmore.

Meanwhile, Dunmore, who had received no reply to his instructions that Lewis join him near Chillicothe, had erected a defense, Fort Gower, at the mouth of the Hocking River. Leaving a garrison of about a hundred men at the hastily constructed post, he set out with the remainder of his army for the Shawnee villages. En route he was met by the emissary of Cornstalk, who informed him of the battle of Point Pleasant and of the desire of the Indians to discuss peace terms. Dunmore told Elliott that he would be willing to open discussions and in preparation for the talks established temporary quarters known as Camp Charlotte.

By then Lewis, leaving Fleming in charge of the troops at Point Pleasant, had proceeded with about a hundred men to meet the governor. On his way he encountered a messenger who informed him that Dunmore had already concluded a treaty with the Indians. This news produced a wave of disapproval among Lewis's men, who were determined to chastise the Shawnees and their allies more severely. With difficulty Lewis restrained their impetuous demands to move against the Indians at once. Soon afterward Dunmore, with about fifty men, arrived at Lewis's camp and persuaded the disappointed militia to return to Point Pleasant.

The Treaty of Camp Charlotte, which Dunmore signed with the Indians, was a tentative agreement and by no means a definitive resolution of the conflict between the Indians and the Virginians in the Ohio Valley. Instead, a permanent arrangement was to be worked out the following spring at Pittsburgh. By the terms of the preliminary treaty, the Indians promised to surrender captives taken in their attacks upon trans-Allegheny settlements, to return slaves, horses, and other valuables which they had seized, and to refrain from hunting south of the Ohio River. As a pledge of their sincerity and intentions to abide by the agreement, they provided a number of hostages.

The promise of the Indians to remain north of the Ohio and a decision of Dunmore to add strength to frontier defenses paved the way for a renewed advance into Kentucky and other trans-Allegheny regions. Upon returning to Williamsburg, the governor posted a garrison of seventy-five men under John Connolly at Fort Dunmore. Replacing the small defense erected at the mouth of the Kanawha by Andrew Lewis was Fort Blair, a "palisaded rectangle, about eighty yards long, with blockhouses at two of its corners and cabins for barracks within." Not only did Fort Blair provide cover for settlements in the Kanawha and Greenbrier valleys, but it also afforded encouragement to speculators, surveyors, and settlers to return to Kentucky. The spring of 1775 promised to be a time of unprecedented movement to that beckoning land.

5

Corporate Enterprise and Individual Initiative

THE DEFEAT of the Shawnees at Point Pleasant heralded both a wave of settlement and a surge of corporate activity in Kentucky. One of the first organizations to take advantage of the new conditions was the Ohio Company of Virginia, which had succumbed to the Kentucky craze in 1773. In the summer of 1775 its surveyor, Hancock Lee, and several assistants laid off a 200,000-acre tract in the Bluegrass region and established Leestown near the site of Frankfort. Most of the Ohio Company tract lay on the South Fork of the Licking River and on the North Fork of Elkhorn Creek. The surveyors also located and entered for themselves and their friends thousands of acres, taking care to avoid military surveys made on Elkhorn Creek in 1774 and 1775 by John Floyd.

The activities of the Ohio Company excited deep concern on the part of the Loyal Company. William Crawford, the official superior of Hancock Lee, held a surveyor's commission from the College of William and Mary and was also a deputy of Thomas Lewis, the powerful surveyor of Augusta County. A number of his surveys had been patented to George Washington. The Loyal Company challenged the legality of Crawford's

appointment, and Washington, rather than face a colli-
sion with a rival organization, apparently prevailed
upon the Ohio Company to send Willis Lee, the brother
of Hancock, rather than Crawford, to Kentucky. Willis
Lee, like his brother, had not been deputized by any
county surveyor and his work therefore constituted no
great threat to the Loyal Company. Moreover, with its
influence in both the council and the General Assembly
of Virginia, the latter was able to block efforts by the
Ohio Company to have its surveys validated. Ohio Company surveys thus remained unpatented, and with the
passage of the Land Law of 1779 were opened to en-
tries, warrants, and patents by others.

Of less concern to the Loyal Company were other surveying operations east of the Kentucky River, most of
them under the direction of Pennsylvanians. One of the
parties, led by Robert Patterson and John McClellan, established McClellan's Station, which in time became
the village of Georgetown. Nicholas Cresswell, a young
Englishman who had been engaged to locate lands for
William Murray, a founder of the Illinois Company, also
searched for desirable tracts in Kentucky. At Connells-
ville, Pennsylvania, Cresswell's party was joined by another under James Nourse, and together the two descended the Ohio. In Kentucky Nourse visited both
Harrodsburg and Boonesborough and laid out tracts on a
stream which he believed to be either Eagle Creek or
the headwaters of the Licking. At or near Fish Creek, on
the upper Ohio, young George Rogers Clark, who had
settled there in 1772, joined the Cresswell and Nourse
parties and traveled with them to Kentucky, where he
became a member of Hancock Lee's surveying team.
The surveys made east of the Kentucky River in 1775
were usually in 400-acre plots which might be patented
later as settlement rights.

Although most of the men in Kentucky in the spring
and summer of 1775 were evidently members of surveying groups, permanent settlers also made their appear-

ance. The first of the latter to reach central Kentucky in that year were led by James and Robert McAfee. Leaving the Holston country with their brothers, Samuel and William, David Adams, Samuel McGee, and their servants, Sever Poulson and John Higgins, they reached Boiling Spring on Salt River on March 11 and began to make improvements on lands surveyed by James and Robert in 1773. The claims of the McAfees were less than a mile from Harrodsburg, where log houses built in 1774 by James Harrod and his companions were still standing.

Harrod, too, was among those who returned to Kentucky. Traveling down the Ohio with forty-two men, many of whom had been with him the preceding summer, he again ascended the Kentucky River and reached Harrodsburg about the middle of March. He and his associates had hardly set foot on the soil of their town before they were met by the McAfee brothers, who angrily charged Harrod with failure to respect the surveys made by the McAfees in 1773. Fortunately, the two parties resolved their differences without undue difficulty.

Harrod, the McAfees, and others who settled south of the Kentucky River almost immediately found themselves under the shadow of the most powerful corporate enterprise in frontier Kentucky. The behemoth which momentarily threatened all their claims and improvements sprang from the mind of Judge Richard Henderson, who had only recently retired from the North Carolina bench. Henderson had noted with interest the waning fortunes of the Vandalia scheme and had concluded that another proprietary venture might succeed where it had failed. Anticipating that the definitive agreement to be concluded at Pittsburgh in the spring of 1775 would extinguish the rights of the Shawnees to territory south of the Ohio River and expecting a large population to flow into Kentucky, Henderson knew that the time had come to act, both decisively and swiftly.

Henderson's plans began to take shape with the formation of the Louisa Company in August 1774. Others associated with him in his speculative combine included his law partner, John Williams; Thomas and Nathaniel Hart, merchants and planters; and their friends John Luttrell and William Johnson. Most of them were former Virginians who had taken up residence in or near Hillsborough, North Carolina. Henderson must certainly have been aware of earlier opposition by Governor Dunmore and Indian Superintendent John Stuart to a proposal by Patrick Henry, William Byrd, William Christian, John Page, and Robert Wormeley to purchase Kentucky lands from the Cherokees. Nevertheless, he endeavored to persuade Henry to join him in a new venture in the hope that he and his associates might increase their chances of success.

The lands which Henderson originally hoped to acquire lay south of the Ohio and west of the Kanawha, with a right-of-access route through Cumberland Gap. The Cherokee chiefs told Henderson and Hart that they would be willing to part with the territory if a satisfactory price could be agreed upon. Henderson and his partners were so confident that they could obtain Kentucky that in December 1774 they advertised in Virginia and North Carolina newspapers that they could provide settlers with five hundred acres of land at twenty shillings per hundred acres down and an annual quitrent of two shillings the hundred.

In January 1775 the Louisa Company was reorganized as the Transylvania Company. Shortly afterward, Henderson invited the Cherokees to a great council at Sycamore Shoals on the Watauga. By then the storm clouds of revolution were darkening, and the royal authority, which had placed restrictions upon private purchases of land from the Indians and upon western settlement, was under serious challenge. Should a revolution occur, Henderson reasoned, actual possession of the desired territory by the Transylvania Company would constitute a strength not otherwise attainable. In the event that differences between England and the colonies were settled peacefully, Henderson would offer to pay quitrents to the Crown in return for recognition of his proposed new colony. At any rate, Henderson was convinced that boldness might bring rich rewards; timidity could accomplish nothing.

In response to Henderson's invitation to the Cherokees, nearly twelve hundred Indians gathered at Sycamore Shoals. On March 19 Henderson and the chiefs set their signatures to the Treaty of Sycamore Shoals. By its terms the Indians, in return for trading goods valued at £10,000, ceded to the Transylvania Company the territory between the Kentucky River and the highlands south of the Cumberland and a strip of land between the Holston River and the Cumberland Mountains. Perhaps in deference to the claims of the Loyal Company, Henderson decided against the Kanawha boundary. At the same time, the Watauga settlers, who had earlier leased their lands from the Cherokees, converted their lease into a purchase. In addition, Jacob Brown bought two tracts on the Nolichucky River, where he and his followers had taken up residence. Upon conclusion of the agreements, Henderson brought out casks of rum for a celebration seldom equaled on the frontiers.

Not all the Cherokee chiefs were pleased with the treaty. Older leaders, including Attakullakulla, or Little Carpenter, Oconostota, and The Raven, considered the offer made by Henderson to be reasonable since the Cherokee claim to the territory ceded was at best tenuous. Younger men, for whom Dragging Canoe was the spokesman, contended that the goods received were not proportionate to the worth of the lands conveyed to the Transylvania Company. In fact, Dragging Canoe warned Henderson that Kentucky would become a dark and bloody ground.

Henderson lost no time in making the most of his bargain. On the very day that he began his council with the Cherokee chiefs he dispatched Daniel Boone and twenty-eight axmen to blaze a trail along the south bank of the Kentucky River. Choosing not to follow the old Warriors Trail, which led from Cumberland Gap to the mouth of the Scioto, Boone proceeded from Long Island on the Holston to the Cumberland River and thence by way of the Rockcastle River to the Kentucky. In later years this trail would become the route of the famed Wilderness Road.

Ironically, Boone's party had scarcely arrived in central Kentucky when the dire prediction of Dragging Canoe appeared likely to be fulfilled. The danger that lurked amid the sirenic attractions of the Bluegrass was vividly described by Felix Walker, one of Boone's companions. On March 24 Walker gazed entranced at two or three hundred buffalo peacefully gathered at a salt lick and marveled at the beauty of the limestone gorge of the Kentucky River. Only one day later an Indian attack left Captain William Twetty and his Negro slave dead and Walker himself with serious wounds.

Ten days after Boone left Long Island Henderson himself started westward. With him were Nathaniel Hart, John Luttrell, about thirty riflemen, a number of Negro slaves, and a wagon train and packhorses loaded with provisions. At Powell Valley he found that Joseph Martin, a trader, had already established a post on lands lying within the domain of the Transylvania Company. Henderson recognized the usefulness of a way station at that point for settlers moving to Kentucky from Virginia and North Carolina by way of Cumberland Gap. Wisely, he allowed Martin to retain his lands, which he had first settled in 1769 under the aegis of the Loyal Company and had reoccupied in early 1775 after being driven out by Indians.

Before leaving Martin's Station, Henderson was joined by five men from Prince William County, Virginia, led by an amiable Welshman named William Calk. Older accounts, notably that of Humphrey Marshall, contend that a party under Benjamin Logan also

75

joined Henderson in Powell Valley, but, since Logan set out from the Holston region and ended his journey at St. Asaph's rather than at Boonesborough, it is more likely that he traveled in company with John Floyd and a party of surveyors who also departed from the Holston country.

En route Henderson encountered numerous settlers whom Indian attacks had forced to flee central Kentucky. He continued to press on, however, and even sent a message to Boone urging him to stand his ground against any effort to drive him from the Bluegrass region. After he had crossed the Rockcastle River, Henderson met the McAfee brothers, with about eighteen companions. He persuaded most of the men to return to central Kentucky with him, but James McAfee questioned Henderson's ownership of the land and refused to collaborate with him.

Not unexpectedly, other pioneers were deeply concerned over Henderson's claims to Kentucky. Among them were John Floyd and Benjamin Logan. Leaving the Wilderness Road at Hazel Patch, Logan and his companions had taken the trail known as Skaggs's Trace, which led toward Harrodsburg. After passing through a country of lush bluegrass, cane, and pea vines, they came upon a knoll overlooking a spring much frequented by buffalo. There, on May 1, 1775, they made camp and set about building cabins and clearing fields for corn and other crops. During the following weeks their numbers were augmented by other immigrants who took the trail southwestward from Hazel Patch. According to tradition, the settlement, which seems to have first been under the direction of John Floyd, was named St. Asaph's by a Welshman, who noted that it was made on the day of the canonization of St. Asaph, a monk living at a monastery on the River Elwy in North Wales. Logan, however, quickly became the recognized leader, and by common usage the settle-

76

ment was known as Logan's Station until it was laid out as a town, whereupon it was named Stanford.

James Harrod also rejected any rights of the Transylvania Company to Kentucky. When Henderson arrived in the Bluegrass region, Harrod was busily at work reclaiming his improvements and rebuilding Harrodsburg. For his own tract he chose a site at Boiling Spring on Dix River. All of Harrod's men contended that their lands lay within Virginia and that Henderson had no legal control over them. In asserting the dominion of Virginia, Harrod, Logan, and others were appealing to a distant authority which for the moment could do but little to counteract the claims of Henderson and the Transylvania Company.

Mutual needs of the Kentucky settlements proved more powerful than temporary divisions; but it took a crisis to convince the first Kentuckians that some orderly government for the individualistic settlements was essential. That crisis came with the arrival of about thirty North Carolinians, who, over the angry protests of earlier residents, began to lay out tracts near Harrodsburg. Henderson seized the opportunity to invite the four stations in Kentucky—Boonesborough, Harrodsburg, St. Asaph's, and Boiling Spring—to send representatives to Boonesborough on May 23 to enact laws for the colony of Transylvania.

Eighteen delegates from the four stations answered Henderson's call. Their deliberations were held in the shade of a large elm tree, where Henderson, with florid oratory, endeavored with no genuine success to play the role of a forest Demosthenes. Without undue dissension they set up a court and a militia system and provided for the punishment of criminals, the preservation of game, and the proper breeding of horses. The instrument of government also envisioned the appointment of judges and sheriffs and annual elections to a colonial assembly. Despite phraseology which seemed to defer to democratic procedures, the document which they drew up in reality vested the government of the Kentucky stations in the Transylvania Company. With some reason, therefore, Henderson continued to look upon Transylvania as a proprietary colony and upon himself as the proprietor.

During the summer of 1775 Harrodsburg, Boonesborough, Boiling Spring, and St. Asaph's began to take on an air of permanence. Most of the immigrants who arrived from North Carolina and southwestern Virginia followed Henderson to Boonesborough. Harrodsburg also continued to receive fairly numerous accretions. Immigrants entering Kentucky by way of the Ohio River usually took the trail southward from Limestone to Boonesborough or set out either from the mouth of the Kentucky or the Falls of the Ohio for Harrodsburg. The most southerly of the stations, St. Asaph's, drew most of its settlers from those moving westward by way of Hazel Patch. By the end of 1775 the western segment of the Wilderness Road, connecting Hazel Patch with the Falls of the Ohio by way of St. Asaph's and Harrodsburg, was as much traveled as the portion leading from Hazel Patch to Boonesborough.

Statistics on the number of residents in Kentucky in the summer of 1775 are at best sensible estimates. Counting the forty-two men who had returned to Kentucky with James Harrod, there were probably about three hundred persons residing in the Bluegrass region, most of them at the four stations which had been established. Other pioneers apparently, ventured out on their own. Isaac Campbell and Benjamin Pettit located near St. Asaph's; Richard Calloway, Flanders Calloway, and James Estill were on Otter Creek; and John Hinkston and John Martin were on the South Fork of the Licking River. William Gillespie had taken up a claim on Boone's Creek, and James Knox, a former Long Hunter, had built a cabin on Beargrass Creek. Squire Boone had left Harrodsburg for a time in order to stake out a claim in present Shelby County. During the summer a number of pioneers, among them Daniel Boone and Benjamin Logan, returned to older settlements for their families. Many of the men actually in Kentucky, therefore, were probably members of surveying and land-seeking parties, such as those of John Floyd on the Kentucky and Elkhorn Creek and Thomas Slaughter on the Green River.

Although the danger from Indians generally increased during the summer of 1776, occupation of Kentucky continued without serious disruption. William Whitley located on Cedar Creek, about two miles west of Crab Orchard, and his brother-in-law, George Clark, took up lands not far away. Joseph, George, Morgan, William, Samuel, and James Bryan settled on the North Fork of the Elkhorn. Others who had established habitations included Jesse Benton on Silver Creek, John Todd on the West Branch of Hickman's Creek, John Strode near the headwaters of the South Fork of the Licking, and James Strode on Howard's Creek. John Floyd, John Bowman, and Leonard Helm had also made settlements in central Kentucky.

On July 14, 1776, a narrow escape from tragedy drew attention to the need for more adequate protection for the Kentucky settlements. That afternoon Betsey and Frances Calloway, the daughters of Richard Calloway, and Jemima, the second daughter of Daniel Boone, went for a boat ride on the Kentucky River in the only canoe at Boonesborough. At a bend in the river below the station the current carried them to the opposite shore and they were captured by six Indians. A pursuit party was delayed for lack of a boat with which to cross the river, and when night came on it had traveled only five miles. At daybreak it resumed the chase and after great difficulty overtook the Indians before they reached the Licking River. The pursuers killed three of the Indians, all Shawnees, but the other three, Cherokees, escaped. Nevertheless, they succeeded in rescuing the three girls, all of whom were unharmed.

News of the incident accelerated defense measures at all the Kentucky stations. Work on the fort at Boonesborough, begun soon after the arrival of Henderson the previous year, had languished, but it was now speeded to completion. The defenses at Harrodsburg and Royal Spring on Elkhorn Creek were also strengthened. Yet, even these measures were insufficient for the security of Kentuckians caught between angry Shawnees on the north and disgruntled Cherokees on the south. Within a week after the capture of the girls at Boonesborough, John Hinkston's settlement on the South Fork of the Licking River broke up as families sought safety elsewhere. Benjamin Logan temporarily gave up the idea of building a fort at St. Asaph's and moved, with several families, to Harrodsburg. Also seeking security at Harrodsburg were William Whitley, George Clark, and a few families from Crab Orchard. Numerous other pioneers who had boldly established solitary residences remote from more densely settled centers also abandoned their homes for the safety of greater numbers.

By the summer of 1776 real fear existed among residents of Kentucky and other trans-Appalachian areas that the Indians northwest of the Ohio River would give up their neutral position and join the British. For the Kentucky settlers such a decision could mean catastrophe. As defense needs began to assume a paramount place in their thinking, many residents concluded that only a vigorous assertion of authority over Kentucky by the government of Virginia could afford them the measure of protection needed; Judge Henderson, they believed, could not.

Despite the harmony that had prevailed at the Boonesborough meeting in May 1775, there was deep-seated antipathy to Henderson's claims to ownership of Kentucky, which defense needs helped to sharpen. Frontiersmen generally rejected the two basic concepts in the Transylvania scheme—the establishment of a proprietary colony and a feudal land system. Although

Henderson had the recent example of the near success of the Vandalia promoters before him, he must have known that the idea of proprietary rule had been rejected in colony after colony and was by 1775 completely anachronistic in American society. Moreover, the feudal system which he envisioned had seldom worked where land was abundant and a sparse population aspired to hold it in fee simple.

Opponents of Henderson never built their case upon rejection of the idea of a privileged class based upon land ownership. What many of them really desired was that they constitute the privileged class. Tolerating Henderson's intrusion out of necessity, they were convinced that the best method of assuring their own success must entail a vigorous assertion of Virginia authority over Kentucky. Among those who became leaders in the opposition to Henderson was George Rogers Clark, a fiery, red-haired Virginia surveyor, who first visited the western country in 1772, when he made a settlement at the mouth of Fish Creek, a few miles south of Wheeling. Clark was among the first surveyors to reach Kentucky in 1773. In the following year he and his associates were driven from Kentucky by hostile Indians. Shortly afterward Clark served as a captain in Dunmore's War, which broke the power of the Shawnees in 1774. With the defeat of the Indians, he returned to Kentucky and was already there by the time that Boone and Henderson founded Boonesborough. He was engaged in making surveys at present Leestown, near Frankfort, at the time that Henderson held the council at Boonesborough and did not take part in its deliberations.

Clark's contacts with Harrodsburg could hardly have left him unaware that the mood in that settlement was rapidly changing from one of tolerating Henderson's claims to one of defiance. The following winter he returned to Virginia, where he also heard prominent officials denounce the pretensions of the Transylvania

Company. In Kentucky again in the spring of 1776, he advised the residents of Harrodsburg to lodge a protest with the General Assembly of Virginia. Upon his recommendation, Harrod, Abraham Hite, Jr., and eighty-six other persons signed a petition in which they declared that they had come to Kentucky because of reports of good land and that they were greatly alarmed at the actions of men who claimed proprietorship and increased the price of land from thirty to fifty shillings for each hundred acres. Specifically, they called upon the General Assembly to take immediate steps to restore harmony among the Kentucky settlements.

With indignation against Henderson mounting, the independent settlers at Harrodsburg acted more decisively. Directing their moves were Harrod, Hite, and John Gabriel Jones, a young attorney. Clark was away making surveys, but he knew of the events. Styling themselves "a Respectable Body of Prime Rifle Men," they endeavored to put their best foot forward by beginning their memorial to the legislature with a vigorous proclamation of their loyalty to the American cause and of their hatred of British tyranny. They utterly rejected the claims of Henderson and asked for representation in the General Assembly. Either as evidence of their determination or of the optimism with which they proceeded, they informed the legislature that they had selected Clark and Jones to represent them in that body.

Clark, who had returned from his surveying expedition, and Jones left at once for Williamsburg. Traveling by way of St. Asaph's, or Logan's Station, and Skaggs's Trace, they almost immediately encountered such difficulties that the success of their mission became highly doubtful. Heavy rains drenched their clothing, but they could make no fires lest they attract Indians. Their journey was made all the more arduous by "scald feet," a painful condition prevalent among pioneer hunters. Despite their miseries, they pressed on and at last crossed

82

Cumberland Gap. Clark tried to cheer his weary companion with the assurance that they would find rest and succor when they reached Martin's Station. The spirits of both men sank, however, when they arrived there and found the post deserted, with evidence that Indians had forced its abandonment.

Expecting an immigrant party from Virginia to pass Martin's Station en route to Kentucky within the next eight or ten days, Clark and Jones concluded that they had best take refuge in one of the remaining cabins and await the coming of assistance. In order to avoid surprise by Indians, they burned the stockade surrounding the cabins. They also laid in a barrel of water, corn from one of the cribs, and meat from a hog, which, to their good fortune, they found running loose inside the stockade. With rifles, sabers, and two braces of pistols, they were prepared for almost any attack short of a storming of their fortress.

One night Clark and Jones heard sounds which they believed were made by Indians. Happily, they discovered that their visitors were former residents who had returned from the Clinch Valley settlements, to which they had fled, for articles they had left behind. The next morning Clark and Jones accompanied them to the Clinch Valley, where they remained a few days to let their feet heal. When they were able to travel again, they continued on to Fincastle.

Upon their arrival they learned, to their great disappointment, that the General Assembly had adjourned. After some reflection, they agreed that Jones should join an expedition then forming against the Cherokees and that Clark should discuss the situation in Kentucky with Governor Patrick Henry at his home in Hanover County. The governor proved sympathetic to the plight of the Kentuckians and was eager to extend the authority and protection of Virginia over them. He gave tangible evidence of his concern by providing Clark with a letter asking the Executive Council of the colony to furnish five hundred pounds of powder to the Kentucky settlements.

Clark found the Executive Council less cooperative. It was reluctant either to diminish Virginia's meager store of powder or to establish any precedent for providing protection to the settlers of Kentucky, but it offered Clark the powder as a personal loan. Clark rejected that arrangement and warned that if Virginia did not give recognition and protection to the Kentuckians they would be forced to seek them elsewhere. This veiled threat of recognizing Henderson's claim was sufficient to bring the council to Clark's way of thinking, and it provided the gunpowder without any strings attached.

When the General Assembly convened a few weeks later, Clark and Jones presented their credentials. They encountered formidable opposition from Colonel Arthur Campbell, who represented Fincastle County in the House of Delegates, and from Richard Henderson, who used every possible method to prevent their being seated. Henderson fought vigorously for legislative confirmation of his rights emanating from the Treaty of Sycamore Shoals. Nevertheless, on December 6, 1776, the legislature struck a blow at Henderson's claims by creating Kentucky County from the part of Fincastle west of the Big Sandy and its Tug Fork and by accepting Clark and Jones as its delegates.

Efforts of the Transylvania promoters to win concessions and recognition from the Continental Congress met with no greater success. They addressed a memorial to that body asking that it "take the infant Colony of Transylvania into their protection" and chose James Hogg as their delegate to Congress. Hogg found other members, notably Samuel Adams, John Adams, and Thomas Jefferson, unsympathetic to the recognition of a state which embraced territory claimed by Virginia. Moreover, Congress opposed both quitrents and the introduction of slavery, which Transylvania sanctioned.

84

The formation of Kentucky County meant more for the Kentuckians than representation in the Virginia legislature. Of immediate consequence was the appointment of a full complement of militia officers and a commitment on the part of Virginia to defend Kentucky. The militia structure included David Robinson as county lieutenant; John Bowman, colonel; Anthony Bledsoe, lieutenant colonel; George Rogers Clark, major; and John Todd, Benjamin Logan, Daniel Boone, and James Harrod, captains. On authorization of the General Assembly, Clark obtained five hundred pounds of powder at Fort Pitt, but the journey down the Ohio River was so perilous that he was obliged to hide it at several places in the vicinity of Limestone. A small party under John Gabriel Jones was later sent to retrieve it, but it was ambushed by Indians, and Jones and three of his men were killed. Fortunately, a second expedition, led by James Harrod, with Simon Kenton as its chief scout, succeeded in bringing in the much needed powder.

In dealing a deathblow to the claims of Henderson and the Transylvania Company, the General Assembly acted in the spirit of the Revolution. It also gave tangible encouragement to pioneers to continue their movement westward and enabled the Kentucky settlements to attain sufficient strength to survive the war. But it did even more. In taking the necessary steps to ensure the viability of the Kentucky settlements it set the stage for some of the most important frontier campaigns in the war and gave Virginia and the United States added reasons for insisting that the entire Ohio Valley be American rather than English once the conflict came to a close.

6

The Revolutionary
War Years

Pioneers who took the trails and watercourses westward to Kentucky and other transmontane regions in the spring and summer of 1775 were keenly aware of the momentous events taking place in faraway Massachusetts. The arduous work of carving homes from a wilderness and the exigencies of pioneer life, nevertheless, tempered their excitement over the political upheaval then loosening the very foundations of the British Empire. For Kentuckians, the simple, human urge to possess land was as overpowering as the will of nations, either established or in the making. At the same time they were mindful of the increasing danger from Indians north of the Ohio River, whose determination to retain hunting grounds south of that stream had not been permanently stifled by their defeat at Point Pleasant the preceding autumn.

Among the first to perceive the effects of the outbreak of hostilities between England and the colonies upon the trans-Appalachian region was Lord Dunmore. Abandoning his aggressive western policies, which had been frowned upon by Lord Dartmouth, as well as by Sir William Johnson and John Stuart, the Indian superintendents, Dunmore immediately set about to make the

Indians allies of the British. In June John Connolly, his agent at Fort Dunmore, conferred with chiefs of tribes north of the Ohio River, but he succeeded in obtaining pledges of friendship only from the Delawares and a few Mingo chiefs. Shortly afterward Dunmore ordered the disbanding of the garrisons of Fort Dunmore, Fort Fincastle, and Fort Blair. By this move he sought to allay tribal fears of British power, gain greater flexibility in deploying his militia, and expose the frontiers to dangers which would force the Americans to divert part of their strength from other battlefronts.

Confronted with this threat to her expansion into the Ohio Valley and perhaps even her claim to trans-Appalachian territory, Virginia acted with decisiveness and dispatch. On August 7 her newly formed Convention responded to urgent pleas from frontier residents by sending a hundred men under Captain John Neville from Winchester to Fort Pitt, previously known as Fort Dunmore. More important, the House of Burgesses, at its final session, had named a commission consisting of Thomas Walker, Andrew Lewis, James Wood, John Walker, and Adam Stephen to treat with the Indians. At great personal risk, Wood visited the Indian villages, where he held preliminary discussions and persuaded tribal chiefs to attend a conference at Pittsburgh.

With representatives of the central Indian department, created by the Continental Congress, acting as little more than observers, the Virginia commissioners succeeded in winning Indian assent to the Treaty of Pittsburgh in October. By its terms most of the tribes north of the Ohio, among them the Shawnees, Delawares, Mingoes, Senecas, Wyandots, Pottawattomis, and Ottawas, accepted the Ohio River as the boundary between the Indian country and areas open to settlement and promised that they would remain neutral in the conflict between England and her American colonies. Although isolated Indian attacks and occasional forays of considerable magnitude punctuated an increas-

87

ingly fragile peace, pioneers continued to stream across the Appalachians, many of them to central Kentucky.

Kentucky settlers also found encouragement in the early exposure and suppression of Loyalist activities on the upper Ohio. On November 20, 1775, colonial authorities arrested John Connolly, Dunmore's close associate, who was secretly planning to gather an army of British and Indians at Detroit for a major attack upon Fort Pitt. Success of his plans, which envisioned cutting the colonies in two, hinged in part upon support from substantial numbers of Loyalists, whom Connolly believed could be found among residents of the upper Ohio and from those who, indifferent to the issues of the war, might be won over by offers of generous land grants. Had Connolly's plan succeeded, Kentucky pioneers could have suffered dire consequences; its failure perhaps contributed to their survival during the ensuing months.

Yet, paradoxically, the growth of the Kentucky settlements was without doubt partly behind the mounting disaffection of the Indians. With attacks upon the settlers increasing in both frequency and ferocity, there seemed in the summer of 1776 a danger that some of the tribes, particularly the Wyandots and Ottawas, would defect to the British. When discussions in the Continental Congress of an expedition against Detroit proved but a dream without substance, Virginia extended her defense perimeter southward from Fort Pitt and Fort Fincastle to the mouth of the Kanawha. There Matthew Arbuckle built Fort Randolph to replace Fort Blair, which had been burned the preceding year by marauding Shawnees. At the close of 1776 she assumed responsibility for the protection of the Kentucky settlements by creating Kentucky County and by authorizing George Rogers Clark to procure powder from Fort Pitt for their defense.

By the beginning of 1777, which was to be one of the bloodiest years ever experienced in frontier history, relations between the Americans and the Indians had so degenerated that the more isolated settlements of Kentucky had broken up, and residents were living at the three forts at Harrodsburg, Boonesborough, and McClellan's. Located on the northeast side of the Kentucky River, the latter was the smallest and most exposed of the stations. On January 30, following the death of John McClellan, its garrison was disbanded and its residents moved to Harrodsburg. Meanwhile, at St. Asaph's Benjamin Logan and others were completing a fort which soon provided protection for a small number of families in the southern Bluegrass. The forts at Harrodsburg and Boonesborough sheltered Logan's Fort from attack by northern Indians, but it was vulnerable to assault by southern tribes.

Clearly, the defense posture of Kentucky at that time left much to be desired. About half of the fighting men in Kentucky were at Harrodsburg, where about forty families were accommodated. A committee of safety for the Kentucky settlements, with Hugh McGary of Harrodsburg as its chairman, appealed to Governor Henry for protection against the Indians. Fortunately, with the creation of Kentucky County, a militia had been organized, with Colonel John Bowman in charge but with George Rogers Clark serving as the ranking officer in Kentucky pending Bowman's arrival from Botetourt County. On March 5 militia were mustered at the three forts under Captains John Todd, James Harrod, Daniel Boone, and Benjamin Logan. Additional precautions were taken by selecting two scouts from each fort to keep watch over the territory between the forts and the Ohio River.

Defense preparations at the Kentucky stations came none too soon. On the very next day after the militia muster Indians appeared in central Kentucky in considerable numbers. Their first victims were Thomas Moore and William Ray, the latter a stepson of Hugh McGary, who were working at Shawnee Spring, about five miles from Harrodsburg. Most of the attacks during the ensuing weeks were minor and confined to the vicinity of Harrodsburg and Boonesborough. Perhaps the most important was an assault upon Boonesborough, which left one man dead and Daniel Boone, John Todd, Isaac Hite, and Michael Stoner wounded. Yet, so fraught with danger was life outside the forts that hunters in search of buffalo and other game were forced to set out during the night in order to avoid detection by lurking Indians.

With a total strength of only 121 fighting men, eighty-four of whom were at Harrodsburg, twenty-two at Boonesborough, and fifteen at Logan's Fort, the Kentucky settlers dreaded the approach of summer. And well they might have. Their assumption in late May that the Indians had left the Bluegrass was suddenly shattered. On the morning of May 30 Ann Logan, Esther Whitley, and a Negro woman named Molly, accompanied by four men, left Logan's Fort for the purpose of milking cows not far from the stockade. Suddenly a band of Indians who had lain in wait in a thick cane-brake opened fire upon them. One man, William Hudson, was killed and scalped, and another, Burr Harrison, was left for dead near the walls of the fort. John Kennedy suffered four bullet wounds, but he, James Craig, and the women succeeded in reaching safety.

The experience of Harrison well illustrates the horrors of a frontier Indian attack. After lying inert outside the fort for more than half a day, Harrison was seen to move slightly. An investigation disclosed that he was conscious but weak from loss of blood. Nevertheless, any attempt to move him inside the stockade might excite the attention of Indians still about. Yet, to leave the wounded man out after nightfall would almost certainly result in his being tomahawked and scalped. At dusk, therefore, Logan, rolling a large bag of wool in front of himself as a shield, crawled toward Harrison. Upon reaching him, Logan abandoned the bag of wool, lifted Harrison to his shoulders, and ran to the fort. The Indians fired upon him, but their first bullet struck the wall near the gate, and Logan and Harrison gained safety before another could be fired. On June 1 the Indians, some fifty in number, departed. Twelve days later Harrison died of the wounds that they had dealt him.

Relief for central Kentucky was essential. On June 6 Benjamin Logan, probably accompanied by James Harrod and a few men from Harrodsburg, set out for the Holston settlements to enlist their aid, but the mission proved fruitless. Assistance, however, was soon on the way. Responding to earlier appeals by Colonel John Bowman, Virginia authorities authorized the newly appointed lieutenant of Kentucky County to raise one hundred militia in Botetourt and Montgomery counties and to proceed to Kentucky. If this force was deemed adequate to the protection of the settlements, it was to remain there; if not, Bowman was directed to escort the Kentuckians to "some interior and secure parts of the country." James Harrod met the militia near Cumberland Gap and guided them to Hazel Patch, where the Wilderness Road forked. From there Bowman continued on to Boonesborough, which he reached on August 1.

Despite the hopes raised by the arrival of Bowman, grimmer days lay ahead for the Kentucky stations. Taking advantage of the increasing fury of the western tribes, British authorities set about to make use of the Indians in their strategy for 1777. Central to their plans were three expeditions, launched from Canada, Fort Oswego, and New York, under the command of John Burgoyne, Barry St. Leger, and William Howe, respectively, with the object of severing New England from the remainder of the states. To enhance the likelihood of success of this three-pronged offensive, Henry Hamilton, the lieutenant governor of England's northwest provinces and commandant at Detroit, was instructed to convene a council of tribal leaders north of the Ohio and to induce them to join the British. Hamilton succeeded in winning over the Ottawa and Chippewa chiefs and some of the Wyandots and Mingoes, but he was unable to secure pledges of support from the Delawares and Shawnees. In July he dispatched fifteen war parties to the frontiers, some of them to Kentucky.

While brandishing the sword, Hamilton also extended the olive branch to settlers in the backcountry. To those who would desert the American cause and present themselves at a British post he offered food, lodging, and humane treatment. Those willing to take up arms against the Americans and serve in the British forces until the end of the war were promised pay equal to the amount they would have received in American service and two hundred acres of land. Hamilton's proposals were not without their attractions. In southwestern Pennsylvania and northern West Virginia Loyalists created such a "frantic scene of mischief" that Colonel Zackquill Morgan of Monongalia County enlisted five hundred militia to suppress their activities. At St. Asaph's Benjamin Logan so feared the effects of Hamilton's proclamation upon weary and apprehensive settlers that he tried to conceal it from them. About this time a number of well-known frontier figures, including Simon Girty, Matthew Elliott, and Alexander McKee, defected to the British.

Although the defeat at Saratoga on October 17 doomed British plans for 1777, they and the Indians achieved greater success in the Ohio Valley. The largest of their attacks was launched against Fort Henry, at Wheeling, on September 1, when about two hundred Wyandots and Mingoes, accompanied by a few Delawares and Shawnees, lured about half the garrison outside the walls of the fort and killed twenty-three of them. Later that month they ambushed Captain William Foreman and a reconnoitering party south of Wheeling, killing Foreman and twenty of his men. Hardly a locality escaped some blow. Within six months after Hamilton had sent out his war parties he had received seventy-seven prisoners and 129 scalps. Brigadier General Edward Hand, who had arrived at Fort Pitt on June 1 with orders from the Continental Congress to coordinate all defenses on the upper Ohio, was forced to give up plans for an invasion of the Indian towns, particularly those of the Wyandots and the Pluggy's Town confederacy, and to use his limited manpower for defense of exposed areas.

Winter, normally a season of restricted military activity, brought no respite to the upper Ohio Valley. In early November Cornstalk, the Shawnee chief, his son Elinipsico, and their companions were killed at Fort Randolph while presumably on a peaceful mission. Such an event was almost certain to invite retaliation. In February 1778 Hand, hoping to relieve a critical shortage of ammunition, led five hundred men to the mouth of the Cuyahoga River, where the British had reportedly established a powder magazine, but he succeeded only in killing three old Indians and capturing two squaws and in earning for his expedition the derisive appellation of the "Squaw Campaign." On May 16 about three hundred Indians, mostly Wyandots and Mingoes, tried unsuccessfully to reduce Fort Randolph and then moved on to the Greenbrier region, where an assault upon Fort Donnelly proved equally futile.

The intensification of Indian attacks, together with their coordination by British officials, aggravated the difficulties normally a part of pioneer life and contributed to shortages of vital supplies, particularly salt. Residents of central Kentucky sometimes went as far as Drennon's Lick for salt, but the risks of visiting the Blue Licks on the Licking River were generally considered too great. On October 14, 1777, the council of Virginia approved a proposal of John Bowman that it construct a fort at Drennon's Lick to protect saltmakers who might thereby supply the Monongahela country as well as the central Kentucky stations, but the fort apparently was never built. So critical was the shortage of salt that a

93

number of Kentuckians, among them Benjamin Logan, even proposed to the General Assembly that it take the socialistic step of making the salt springs public property if their owners had not taken measures to produce that essential commodity.

The salt shortage resulted in an unfortunate experience for Daniel Boone, but one which undoubtedly prevented the fall of Boonesborough later. In February 1778, while acting as a hunter for a salt-making party at Blue Licks, Boone was captured by a band of Shawnees. Fearing that the Indians were bound for Boonesborough, which was in no condition to withstand an assault, Boone decided to divert the attention of the Shawnees to the saltmakers. He struck a bargain with Chief Blackfish whereby Boone agreed to lead the Indians to the saltmakers in return for a promise by Blackfish to treat them as prisoners of war. Roundly condemned by the Detroit-bound saltmakers as a traitor, Boone had gambled correctly that their capture would at least temporarily spare Boonesborough.

Winter passed, and after a relatively uneventful spring in which William Whitley's raid upon Shawnee towns excited perhaps the most attention among the Kentucky settlers summer returned. With it came preparations for a large-scale Indian attack upon Boonesborough. While a captive in the Miami villages, Daniel Boone learned of the plan. Knowing that the residents of the fort must be warned, Boone contrived to escape from an Indian salt-making party on June 16, 1778, and, spurred by a conviction that the Kentucky stations faced an unprecedented peril, he reached Boonesborough, 160 miles distant, in only four days. Upon receiving his warning, residents quickly put the fort in a state of readiness. When days and then weeks passed without any sign of Indians, however, some of the occupants began to suspect Boone of giving them false information. Then, on the night of September 6, eleven weeks after Boone's arrival, Blackfish and Dagniaux DeQuindre, his

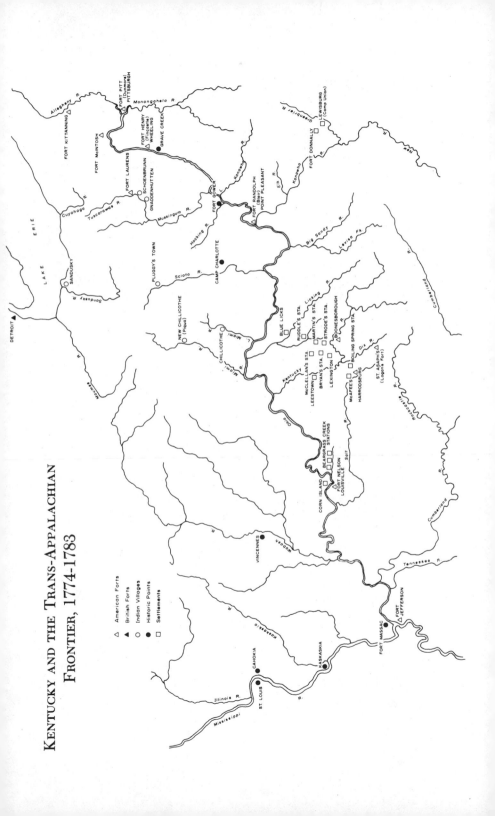

KENTUCKY AND THE TRANS-APPALACHIAN
FRONTIER, 1774-1783

△ American Forts
▲ British Forts
○ Indian Villages
● Historic Points
□ Settlements

French-Canadian mentor, appeared before the gates of Boonesborough.

The attempt of the Indians to reduce Boonesborough provides one of the most colorful events in the history of pioneer Kentucky. After failing to gain entry into the fort by means of crude diplomacy, the Indians stormed its gates. When their efforts proved unavailing, they tried to set the fort afire, but again they were foiled. They then resorted to digging a tunnel from the Kentucky River to a point within the stockade. The sustained effort required for such an undertaking, however, was foreign to the tactics of warriors who must live off the land during military campaigns. Recognizing the futility of their plan, the weary and impatient Indians admitted their defeat. On the rainy night of September 16, ten days after they had first invested the fort, the attackers withdrew. Boonesborough had been saved.

The determined defenders of Boonesborough did more than preserve their own station and others of central Kentucky; they enabled highly secret plans conceived earlier in 1778 by George Rogers Clark to reach fruition. After leaving the Bluegrass the preceding October, Clark had laid before Governor Henry a proposal for an expedition against the former French posts in the Illinois country. Not only did the governor approve the scheme, but the General Assembly provided funds in a measure so ambiguously phrased that only its sponsors knew its real purpose. Clark was transferred from the Kentucky County militia to the Virginia Line, with the rank of lieutenant colonel, and given two sets of instructions. His public orders were "to enlist Seven Companies of men officered in the usual manner" and to proceed to Kentucky, where he and his men would remain for three months. Privately, he was instructed to attack the British post at Kaskaskia.

Forbidden to recruit east of the Blue Ridge, Clark drew most of his men from the Monongahela Valley. Despite the prospects of bounties of three hundred acres of land, which Thomas Jefferson, George Wythe, and George Mason were urging the General Assembly to provide the participants, enlistments for Clark's expedition were slow. When he left Pittsburgh Clark had only about 150 men instead of the five hundred he had expected.

Clark proceeded down the Ohio to the mouth of the Kentucky, where he contemplated building a fort to serve as a base for the Illinois campaign. The post would have afforded protection to Boonesborough and St. Asaph's on the Kentucky River as well as to Harrodsburg, across a dividing ridge, on Salt River. But it would have been too far from the Illinois country, and Clark rejected the site in favor of Corn Island, opposite the mouth of Beargrass Creek and a short distance above the Falls of the Ohio.

At the mouth of the Kentucky Clark was joined by Captain John Montgomery with a number of men from the Kentucky stations, among whom were Simon Kenton and William Whitley. Not wishing to deprive central Kentucky of needed militia, Clark sent some of Montgomery's men back home. In addition, he appointed James Trabue commissary for the three existing stations and a new settlement at the Falls of the Ohio made by pioneers who had accompanied Clark down the Ohio.

Before setting out from Corn Island on June 26, 1778, Clark, for the first time, informed his men, now numbering 175, of the purpose of his expedition. At Fort Massac, an abandoned French post ten miles below the mouth of the Tennessee, Clark and his army hid their boats and continued the remaining 120 miles overland. After losing their way under circumstances which aroused unjustified suspicions of treachery on the part of their guide, John Saunders, Clark and his men reached the Kaskaskia River on July 4. That night they marched into the town of Kaskaskia, captured the Chevalier Philippe de Rastel Rocheblave, the British commandant, and took possession without firing a shot.

Clark's display of temperance and good judgment in his moment of victory combined with news of the recent alliance between the United States and France to win him the support of the French population. By a skillful mixture of bluster and tact he also won over most of the Indian tribes of the locality. Shortly afterward Captain Joseph Bowman took possession of Cahokia, St. Philippe, and Prairie du Rocher, and Father Pierre Gibault prepared the way for the surrender of Vincennes to Captain Leonard Helm, who occupied nearby Fort Sackville.

The American conquest of the Illinois country presented Lieutenant Governor Hamilton with an intolerable situation, which threatened the British position in the West. Gathering a force of British, Canadians, and Indians, among whom there were perhaps no more than thirty-three regulars, Hamilton set out by way of the Maumee and Wabash rivers for Vincennes, which he recaptured in a surprise attack in late December. Believing that winter weather and flooded prairie streams would provide sufficient protection for his winter quarters at Fort Sackville, Hamilton allowed the Canadians to return to Detroit and the Indians to go back to their villages. Further military moves would be postponed until spring.

Capitalizing upon the very elements which Hamilton viewed as protection, Clark struck while he yet held an advantage. With 172 men, including French volunteers, he left Kaskaskia for Vincennes, 180 miles away. To prevent the British from escaping down the Ohio, he dispatched to Vincennes a row galley, the *Willing*, armed with two four-pounders and four swivel guns and commanded by John Rogers. Upon arriving at Vincennes, Clark boldly informed the French and Indians that the "Long Knives" had surrounded the town, a ruse that won the support of the former and frightened off the latter. Deprived of these sources of support and unable to use his artillery, the surprised Hamilton was forced to capitulate on February 25, 1779. He and twenty-five of his men were sent to Williamsburg as prisoners of war.

For Clark, the real prize yet remained to be won. Only the capture of Detroit could insure the erosion of British power in the West and relieve the distresses of Kentucky and other trans-Appalachian regions. The summer of 1779, when only about a hundred men were available for the defense of Detroit, would have been the ideal time for an attack upon that post. But Clark well knew that his successes in the Illinois country stemmed from no genuine military superiority and that there had been no real test of strength between the Americans and the British. Moreover, to reach Detroit he would have to pass through territory of hostile Indians amid almost incalculable dangers. With frontier militia ill disposed to leave their families and homes without adequate protection in order to strike at so distant a stronghold, there was little prospect of challenging the British at Detroit.

Despite his inability to crown his western achievements with the capture of the keystone of British western power, Clark's conquests in the Illinois country were not without significant psychological consequences and were partially responsible for the improvement in the American position in 1778 and 1779. They also played an important part in the expansion of settlements in Kentucky. Newcomers continued to arrive at Logan's Fort, or St. Asaph's, and in April 1779 Isaac Ruddle established a station on the Licking River at the site abandoned by John Hinkston and his neighbors in 1776. John Martin led another party from Logan's Fort and founded a settlement on Stoner Creek, a few miles from Ruddle's Station. In April, also, the Bryan brothers, who had staked a claim on the North Fork of Elkhorn Creek in 1776, returned to Kentucky. With them they brought a large party of Virginians and North Carolinians and began construction of one of the largest forts in Kentucky.

The growth of the Kentucky settlements was so steady and promising that John Bowman informed Clark that he could provide three hundred men from Kentucky County for an attack upon Detroit. While Clark was waiting for an opportune time for his proposed expedition, Bowman undertook another which undoubtedly had far greater support among Kentuckians. Believing that most of the attacks upon the Kentucky stations had been made by the Shawnees, Bowman laid plans to strike at their town of Chillicothe on the Little Miami River, between present Xenia and Springfield. At a rendezvous held at the mouth of the Licking River, he assembled nearly three hundred men, drawn from Boonesborough, Harrodsburg, Martin's and Ruddle's stations, and the settlements at the Falls of the Ohio.

At Chillicothe Bowman's men plundered and burned the Indian cabins, but they were unable to gain entry into the council house. Nevertheless, they left the town with considerable booty, including nearly two hundred horses, furs, skins, and silver ornaments. About fifteen miles from Chillicothe, however, they were overtaken by a large party of Indians and forced into a battle which lasted for three hours. Although older accounts have generally treated Bowman's expedition as a failure, more recent investigations have demonstrated that it was not without positive results. Not only did it convince the Shawnees that the Kentuckians could strike swiftly and effectively, but it also contributed to the failure of the British to besiege Fort Laurens on the Tuscarawas River by depriving them of at least two hundred warriors.

Conditions appeared more promising in Kentucky in the late summer of 1779 than at any time since settlements had begun. On August 20 Clark, who had returned from the Illinois country, invited residents from other Kentucky settlements to join in a celebration to be held at Fort Nelson at the Falls of the Ohio, where Clark had established his headquarters. The party began with a jig danced by James and Ann Harrod. Enlivened by ample supplies of rum which Clark had brought with him, it continued for several days and provided a much needed respite from the stern demands of wartime living.

The note of confidence and optimism sounded by the ball gave way to gloomier prospects as the year drew to a close. Contributing to the pall which fell over the western country were the misfortunes of Colonel David Rogers. In the autumn of 1779 Rogers and his men were returning from New Orleans with supplies of gunpowder, medicines, and other needed articles, loaded aboard five batteaux. In addition, Rogers carried important dispatches for Clark. Perilous at best, the journey was, nevertheless, without serious mishap until the party reached the Ohio. On October 4, as Rogers and his men approached an extensive sandbar about three miles below the mouth of the Little Miami River, a large number of Indian rafts suddenly emerged from that stream into the Ohio. Rogers quickly landed his men on the sandbar, where he hoped to ambush the Indians. He was too late. Already, the Indians, several hundred strong and accompanied by Simon Girty, his two brothers, and Matthew Elliott, had observed the approach of the Americans. They immediately surrounded the sandbar and in the ensuing battle killed or captured all but ten of Rogers's men. Among the wounded were a Captain Benham, who was unable to walk, and a man named Watson, who had both arms broken. Fortunately, they found and assisted each other until passing boatmen rescued them.

Worse still, the dispatches that Rogers was to deliver to Clark fell into the hands of the Girtys, who became fully aware of just how tenuous the American foothold in the Illinois country really was. Revelations of the weakness of their position led the Indian tribes, among them the Wyandots, which a few months earlier had begun to court American favor, to turn again to the British. In the following months American influence in the West sank to its lowest ebb.

Despite the setbacks, immigrants continued to pour into Kentucky. In the spring of 1780 three hundred boatloads of settlers arrived at the Falls of the Ohio alone. Many of them remained in the vicinity of Fort Nelson, but others established stations along Beargrass Creek. Unlike older residents, who had been predominantly Virginians and North Carolinians, many of the newcomers were from Maryland and Pennsylvania.

Provision for the defense of the increasing population and expanding frontiers produced deep dissatisfaction among Kentuckians. They applauded the arrival of Colonel George Slaughter with a regiment of 150 men at Fort Nelson, making it the best fortified post in Kentucky, but they criticized Virginia authorities for not sending two regiments, as the General Assembly had authorized. More severely condemned was the departure of Clark with some two hundred men to build a fort about five miles below the mouth of the Ohio River in the land of the Chickasaws, who, unlike the northern tribes, had been no threat to the Kentucky settlers. Increasingly, charges were made that Clark and Virginia officials either failed to understand or cared little about the defense needs of the Kentucky pioneers.

The British took advantage of Clark's absence in constructing Fort Jefferson and a somewhat general pessimism pervading the Ohio Valley settlements to mount two offensives in the spring of 1780. One army, commanded by Emanuel Hesse, was to move south from Mackinac, regain control of the Illinois villages, descend the Mississippi, and recapture West Florida from its Spanish conquerors. Anticipating Hesse's plan, Clark lay in wait at Cahokia. There his presence so overawed Hesse's Indian allies that the British were forced to

Daniel Boone looks out upon Kentucky and a great herd of buffalo.

From Z. F. Smith, *History of Kentucky*

Richard Henderson negotiates the Treaty of Sycamore Shoals with the Cherokees.

Courtesy of the Kentucky Historical Society

Boonesborough

From George W. Ranck, *Boonesborough*

Meeting of the Transylvania Representatives
from the Kentucky Stations at Boonesborough, May 1775

From George W. Ranck, Boonesborough

Benjamin Logan saving Burr Harrison from being scalped

John Floyd
Courtesy of The Filson Club,
Louisville, Kentucky

George Rogers Clark

Isaac Shelby

Courtesy of The Filson Club,
Louisville, Kentucky

Daniel Boone

Courtesy of The Filson Club,
Louisville, Kentucky

Captain Patterson escapes from the Battle of Blue Licks.

move on to St. Louis, where they were received by a withering cannon fire. In disgrace, Hesse beat a retreat to Mackinac.

The other expedition, under Captain Henry Bird, enjoyed greater success. In April Bird left Detroit with 150 white men, about a thousand Indians, and six pieces of artillery. With him was Simon Girty, who was in charge of a band of Wyandots. Bird planned to strike at Fort Nelson, but en route he discovered that the Licking River was in full flood and that he could ascend it to the central Kentucky stations. At present Falmouth he was forced to take to land. With the necessity of clearing a wagon road and transporting his cannon intact, he was eleven days in reaching Ruddle's Station, his first objective. The firing of two cannon cracked the will of the defenders of the post to resist, and Captain Isaac Ruddle had little difficulty in prevailing upon them to surrender. Their decision was made easier by a promise by Bird that they would be well treated. Bird, however, proved incapable of restraining his Indian allies.

Following the victory at Ruddle's Station, Bird hastened to Martin's Station, which capitulated a week later. By then the Licking River was falling rapidly and it would soon be impossible to transport the cannon by water. Perhaps also distressed by the excesses of the Indians, Bird, with about a hundred prisoners, decided to leave Kentucky and return to Detroit.

Once the immediate danger was over, Kentuckians began to demand revenge against the British and Indians. Upon learning of the attacks, Clark hastened back to Kentucky and at Harrodsburg organized a retaliatory expedition. On August 1 nearly a thousand men gathered at the mouth of the Licking River, the appointed place of rendezvous. Dividing his force into two sections, which he placed under the command of William Linn and Benjamin Logan, Clark set out for the Shawnee country, with Simon Kenton leading the way. Delayed by the necessity of clearing a road for moving his artillery, he reached the Shawnee villages on August 6. Finding the towns deserted, the Kentuckians burned cabins and destroyed crops and orchards. They then moved up the Big Miami to Piqua, where the Indians, led by Simon Girty, had prepared to make a stand. When confronted with Clark's cannon fire, however, they broke and ran. Again Clark laid waste dwellings and crops in the belief that dire want among the tribes would lessen the likelihood of future attacks upon the Kentucky stations. His display of strength, nevertheless, had been no more impressive than that of Bird, and the Indians were not yet ready to rally to the American side.

Clark continued to dream of capturing Detroit. His hopes soared when he was named a brigadier general of Virginia troops, with headquarters at Louisville, and instructed to gather a force of two thousand men. The militia, as usual, refused to leave their homes and families to take part in the campaign. The only county of northwestern Virginia to fill its quota of men was Hampshire, which had little to fear from the Indians. When Clark mustered his men at Wheeling he had only four hundred, and desertions were so numerous that he decided to move on down the Ohio without waiting for about a hundred men from Westmoreland County, Pennsylvania, under Archibald Lochry. At the mouth of the Licking River, Lochry's force was ambushed by a large party of Indians, led by Alexander McKee and Joseph Brant, the Mohawk chieftain. Sixty-four of Lochry's men were killed and the other forty-two were captured.

Kentuckians were no more inclined to join an expedition against Detroit than were residents of northwestern Virginia. Like other frontier settlers they took a somewhat myopic view of the war in the West. Moreover, many had lost confidence in Clark. The abandonment of Fort Jefferson appeared as an admission of a costly mistake, which had served only to precipitate an uprising among the Chickasaws. Clark's latest scheme for a fleet of row galleys on the Ohio seemed equally ill conceived. Moreover, the danger to the Kentucky settlements from the northern tribes was yet very real. In March 1781 Colonel William Linn and two other militia officers were killed on Beargrass Creek. The following month Squire Boone and several families who were moving to Louisville were attacked. A retaliatory expedition of thirty mounted men under Colonel John Floyd was ambushed and half of them lost their lives. Reluctantly, Clark was forced to give up his plans for attacking Detroit and to concentrate his efforts upon improving the defenses of Fort Nelson. Again his actions drew criticism, this time for neglecting the needs of the Bluegrass region.

News of the British defeat at Yorktown once again lit the fires of hope for Kentuckians that peace might return to their beleaguered land, but the surrender of Cornwallis did not end the war west of the Appalachians. There hostilities with the British and Indians continued for more than a year. In March 1782 a band of Wyandots struck at Strode's Station, about twenty miles from Boonesborough, where they killed two men, wounded another, and captured several Negroes. Although unable to pursue the Indians, the survivors spread the alarm and enabled other stations to prepare for attack. Upon learning of the assault upon Strode's Station, Benjamin Logan dispatched fifteen men from St. Asaph's to Estill's Station, near Richmond, and placed Captain James Estill and his men on duty. With twenty-five men, Estill trailed the Indians into Fayette County and on the morning of March 22 overtook them near present Mount Sterling. In the ensuing battle, fought in a densely wooded field on the banks of Hinkston Creek, Estill, Lieutenant John South, and six of the men lost their lives.

Most Kentuckians believed that the incursions in the spring of 1782 were but the preliminaries to a full-scale invasion. John Floyd was convinced that the British

105

planned to capture Fort Nelson and then establish their dominion over all of Kentucky. In anticipation of a major thrust southward by the British and Indians, Clark rushed the defenses of Fort Nelson to completion. In addition, by July 6 he had launched the first of a fleet of gunboats with which he proposed to patrol the section of the Ohio River between the Licking and the Miami. Seventy-three feet long, with forty-six oars and a complement of 110 men, the *Miami* was designed to carry eight cannon, ranging from one to six pounds in size.

Fortunately for Clark, British intelligence was no better than his own. Interpreting the burst of military activity in Kentucky as probable preparation for an invasion of Canada, Captain William Caldwell posted troops between Detroit and the Kentucky border, a basically defensive move which hardly pointed to a major thrust against Kentucky. The British took heart from the costly defeat on June 4 and 5 of an American force under Colonel William Crawford, which had marched against the Delawares and Wyandots on the Sandusky in what they construed as a possible preliminary to the anticipated invasion.

Although Caldwell and Alexander McKee were apparently aware of tentative plans for a drive by Clark into the Indian country in conjunction with a similar move from Fort Pitt by General William Irvine, they apparently concluded, with the approach of autumn, that the threat of an invasion of Canada had been exaggerated. After adding some two hundred men to the defenses of Detroit, Caldwell and McKee, with about 1,100 men, took the offensive, ostensibly for the purpose of collecting prisoners from whom they might obtain more precise knowledge of the American plans.

Caldwell and McKee originally planned to attack Fort Henry, at Wheeling, but they changed course upon receiving a report that Clark was at the mouth of the Licking River with two gunboats. When the information proved false, most of the Indians, unprepared for a long campaign and despairing of action, deserted Caldwell. With only about three hundred men left, mostly Indians and some Canadian rangers, Caldwell and McKee decided to strike at the Kentucky settlements rather than return empty-handed.

Bryan's Station, about five miles north of Lexington, felt the first blow. On the morning of August 16 the British and Indians invested the fort. Two men were able to slip out, evade detection by the enemy, and make their way to Lexington for help. With about thirty militia from Lexington and another ten from Boone's Station, Major Levi Todd rushed to the relief of the besieged post. Seventeen of his men succeeded in entering the fort, but Todd and the remainder had to turn back. Unable to force the defenders of the fort to capitulate, Caldwell and the Indians destroyed livestock and crops outside its walls and then tried unsuccessfully to burn the structure. At last, on the morning of August 17, they withdrew.

Following the attack upon Bryan's Station an alarm was sounded throughout the Bluegrass region. On the morning of August 18 Colonel Stephen Trigg arrived at Bryan's Station with 130 Lincoln County militia. They were joined by Colonel Daniel Boone, Major Levi Todd, and militia from Fayette County, bringing the total strength of the relief forces to 182 men, all mounted. With John Todd, the only county lieutenant present, in command, the militia set out in pursuit of the British and Indians.

Meanwhile, at St. Asaph's Benjamin Logan, who did not learn of the attack until dusk on August 17, assembled 154 men and departed for Bryan's Station. At both Lexington and Bryan's Station he found the residents reassured by the size of the forces under Todd, Trigg, and Boone. Nevertheless, Logan continued on in his decision to add his men to theirs. When he was only about five miles from Bryan's Station he was met by some twenty-five militia in full flight from the battle of

Blue Licks, which their accounts made clear had been a major military disaster. Logan covered their retreat and moved his men back to the vicinity of Bryan's Station and Lexington.

The militia under Todd first sighted Indians at Lower Blue Licks in an area almost enclosed by a horseshoe bend in the Licking River. The Kentuckians crossed the river at the toe of the horseshoe, the only fording place, and advanced in three columns to within sixty yards of the enemy. Trigg commanded the right wing, Major Hugh McGary the center, and Boone the left. Boone's column made the first contact with the Indians, who quickly dropped back about a hundred yards. Unwittingly the militia had advanced into a death trap, which evidence indicates was cleverly contrived by Caldwell and McKee. Scores of Indian warriors suddenly swarmed from their places of concealment, and the ranks of the militia became hopelessly confused. For most of the Kentuckians the only thought was escape, but most avenues to safety had been cut off. In the wild and disorganized fighting Colonels Todd and Trigg, Major Silas Harlan, four captains, five lieutenants, and about sixty privates lost their lives. Blue Licks, with its near catastrophic outcome, replaced the cautious optimism of central Kentucky with gloom and apprehension for the approaching autumn.

Upon hearing of the magnitude of the losses at Blue Licks, Logan ordered out all the Lincoln County militia and on August 23, with 470 men, set out for the Blue Licks. Once he had reached the battle scene he found convincing evidence that the Indians had crossed the Ohio immediately after the engagement. Logan and his men took time to bury in a common grave forty-three stripped and mutilated bodies, not one of which could be positively identified, and sadly returned to Lexington and thence to their homes.

Inevitably, a tragedy of such proportions led to efforts to fasten blame upon someone. Several doubtful accounts made Hugh McGary the villain, charging him with wrecking a council of officers deliberating a course of action and with impetuously precipitating the ill-fated advance across the Licking River. McGary countered with equally dubious accusations against Trigg, whose delay in notifying Logan of the attack at Bryan's Station prevented Logan from overtaking the advance party in time to render it assistance. Colonel Arthur Campbell, the powerful lieutenant of Washington County, who was embittered by the failure of his proposal to create a new state in the West, swung the ax of accusation in all directions. In a report marked by malice and false statements, he declared that "Todd & Trigg had capacity but wanted experience," while Boone, Harlan, and Joseph Lindsay had experience "but were defective in capacity." Logan he described as "a dull, narrow body from whom nothing clever need be expected."

No Kentucky military leader suffered greater abuse than George Rogers Clark, whose past actions were criticized anew by a number of other military officers, among whom were Logan, Boone, Andrew Steel, Levi Todd, Robert Patterson, Benjamin Netherland, and Eli Cleveland. Singled out for attack were his emphasis upon defenses at Louisville, Fort Nelson, Fort Jefferson, and the Illinois posts, his alleged neglect of Bluegrass settlements, his use of row galleys on the Ohio, and his failure to undertake an offensive campaign against the northern Indians. Most central Kentucky residents undoubtedly supported Daniel Boone, the senior officer of Fayette County, who on August 30 called upon the General Assembly to provide five hundred men for the protection of Kentucky. Boone urged that they be placed under the command of the county lieutenants and not under Clark, whose headquarters were a hundred miles west of the Bluegrass settlements and of little use in dealing with Indians to the north.

Military leaders of Kentucky could not allow the

charges and countercharges to obscure the dangers that yet threatened the settlements. Without waiting for permission from Virginia authorities, Clark laid plans for a retaliatory expedition against the Shawnees in the Miami Valley. With the aid of Logan, Floyd, and Boone, the lieutenants of Lincoln, Jefferson, and Fayette counties, respectively, he gathered an army of 1,050 men, which held its rendezvous on November 1 at the mouth of the Licking River. Clark had expected to concert his offensive with another advancing from Fort Pitt under Irvine. By the time that he received word that Irvine would be delayed, Clark was well on his way to the Shawnee town of New Chillicothe, also known as New Piqua, Upper Piqua, and the Standing Stone. Warned of the approach of the Kentuckians, the Indians deserted the town, as well as their villages of McKee's Town and Willston. Clark failed to engage warriors in battle, but he collected a vast amount of plunder and destroyed cabins and crops.

The Treaty of Paris of September 3, 1783, officially ended the war between the United States and England. Even then hostilities between trans-Appalachian pioneers and tribes north of the Ohio did not entirely cease. Although Kentucky settlements, with their rapidly increasing population, were less vulnerable to Indian raids than slower growing trans-Appalachian regions, even there the Indian menace did not disappear until the victory of Anthony Wayne at Fallen Timbers in 1794.

7

The Seeds of
a Commonwealth

THE HARDSHIPS of frontier life never stood in the path of the American pioneer in search of a new beginning, and, unless the odds were truly overwhelming, danger from the Indians seldom proved a deterrent to the inexorable march of population westward. Lands as rich and attractive as those of central Kentucky, moreover, cast a spell of their own. The advance into Kentucky, which had been spurred by the defeat of the Indians at Point Pleasant and the Treaty of Pittsburgh of 1775, developed into a substantial stream with the enactment of the land law of 1779 by the Virginia legislature. By the end of 1783 approximately 12,000 people were living in Kentucky.

Many of the early immigrants of Kentucky had already known the vicissitudes and met the challenges of pioneer life in western Pennsylvania, the Appalachian Valley sections of Maryland and Virginia, and along the waters of the Holston and its tributaries. Out of their experiences they had developed a self-reliance and a self-assurance that were to become characteristic traits of the westering American. They were, generally, a confident and optimistic people, whose buoyancy lightened the burdens of life in their new environment.

The exigencies of frontier life and the ever-present need for defense against the British and Indians absorbed much of the attention of pioneer Kentuckians and undoubtedly slowed their efforts to plant educational, religious, and political institutions. Yet, many were sustained in times of peril and uncertainty by deep religious convictions. Most of them had sprung from families originally staunchly Presbyterian, Anglican, Quaker, Lutheran, or German Reformed. Their denominational ties, however, had been profoundly affected by long neglect of frontier regions by their own churches and by the great religious upheaval of the eighteenth century known as the Great Awakening.

By the time that settlements began to spread into Kentucky the Great Awakening had spread from New England into the middle and southern colonies. The revival stressed evangelistic work, the need for a personal religious experience and conversion by each individual, the truth of the feelings, and the lack of any need for a highly educated ministry. Its chief beneficiaries west of the mountains were the Methodists and Baptists, whose ministers braved every danger in order to carry the gospel to isolated settlers. Less numerous were the Presbyterians and Episcopalians, whose insistence upon a trained ministry prevented them from meeting the religious needs of the people as well as did the Methodists and Baptists.

With a highly democratic organization in which authority was centered in the congregation, an enviable record of leadership in the fight for separation of church and state, and courageous and dedicated ministers, the Baptist Church was ideally suited to the needs of Kentucky pioneers. The establishment of the church in Kentucky was largely the work of Virginians, who provided most of the ministerial leadership. As early as 1776 Thomas Tinsley conducted services at Harrodsburg. In that same year, also, Squire Boone and William Hickman were both serving as itinerant Baptist preachers in

Kentucky. Three years later John Taylor, Joseph Reading, and Lewis Lunsford, all of Virginia, visited Kentucky, but they found the residents so pressed with mundane matters that they considered any sustained revivalistic efforts premature.

As in other trans-Appalachian regions, such as West Virginia and Tennessee, Baptist ministers in Kentucky were relatively slow in organizing congregations. Not until 1781, when a little band of eighteen Baptists met under the shade of a maple tree in Severns Valley, was the first congregation established in Kentucky. Its first pastor, John Garrard, served the church until he was captured and killed by Indians. In 1781, also, the "Traveling Church," led by the Reverend Lewis Craig and Captain William Ellis, moved as a body from Spotsylvania County, Virginia, to Gilbert's Creek, Kentucky. In 1783 Craig organized another congregation five miles south of Lexington on the South Fork of Elkhorn Creek, with members drawn largely from the Gilbert's Creek Church. The preceding year John Taylor, one of the most influential Baptist ministers in early Kentucky and a leading figure in the anti-mission movement in the Baptist Church, settled in Kentucky. By 1785 there were in Kentucky eighteen Baptist churches, nineteen ministers, and three associations. Of the latter, the Elkhorn and Salem associations were made up of Regular Baptist churches, and the South Kentucky Association represented the Separates.

The Presbyterians also founded congregations in Kentucky before the end of the Revolutionary War. Perhaps the first Presbyterian minister in the state was Terah Tamplin, a licentiate from the Hanover Presbytery in Virginia, who arrived in Kentucky in 1780 and later established several congregations. The "Father of Western Presbyterianism," however, was David Rice. During a visit to Kentucky in 1783 in search of lands for his family, Rice was presented with a subscription paper with three hundred signatures requesting him to serve as a Presbyterian minister in Kentucky. He took up his labors there and founded churches at Danville, Cane Ridge, and Dix River. By 1785 there were twelve Presbyterian congregations in central Kentucky. The following year these churches became a part of the Transylvania Presbytery, which included all of Kentucky, the Cumberland region of middle Tennessee, and congregations on the Big and Little Miami rivers in Ohio.

By the close of the Revolutionary War a number of Catholic families had also settled in Kentucky. The first was the Coomes family, who emigrated from Charles County, Maryland, to Harrodsburg in 1775. Other Catholics were soon found at most of the other stations in Kentucky. Through the efforts of a Catholic colonization society, a group of Catholics left Maryland in 1785 and settled in the vicinity of Pottinger's Creek, a few miles from Bardstown. As late as 1787, when there were about fifty Catholic families in Kentucky, there was still no resident priest. Like other pioneers, the Catholics were attracted to Kentucky by the abundance of good land.

Other denominations later to become significant in the religious history of Kentucky established few churches before the end of the Revolutionary War. The growth of Methodism began in 1783 when Francis Clark, a local preacher from Mercer County, Virginia, organized a class at Danville. By 1785 there were sufficient Methodists in Kentucky to cause Bishop Francis Asbury to send James Haw and Benjamin Ogden to serve the newly formed Kentucky Circuit. Yet, when Asbury himself visited Kentucky in 1790, he was forced to admit that "The Methodists do but little here—others lead the way."

Wartime conditions, which slowed the growth of churches, had an even more deleterious effect upon education. Formal schooling apparently began in Kentucky in 1775 when Mrs. William Coomes began a dame school at Fort Harrod. Most, if not all, of the forts provided some elementary education for the children within their vicinity. At McAfee's Fort John May was offering instruction in reading, writing, and arithmetic in 1779. Similar opportunities were available at Boonesborough, where Joseph Doniphan's school had an average of seventeen pupils during the summer of that year. "Wildcat" John McKinney instructed youth at Lexington whenever he was not fighting wildcats and Indians. These fort schools were the antecedents of the "old field" schools, a subscription-type institution common to Kentucky and other trans-Appalachian regions.

The type and quality of education available to Kentucky children were hardly satisfactory for the founding of a republic whose vitality must rest upon the enlightenment of its citizens. The educational deficiencies of Virginia, of which Kentucky was a part, were recognized by Governor Thomas Jefferson, who in 1779 recommended a plan for the education of all children at state expense. Jefferson's proposal, made to the General Assembly, would have provided education to each child commensurate with his industry and talents. It gained some support during the war years, when the fires of patriotism burned brightly, but large landholders declined to saddle themselves with the financial burdens of educating all children, and the idea remained but a dream.

Although the General Assembly of Virginia severely restricted its educational efforts with respect to the general population, it took the first steps in the advancement of education of academic grade in Kentucky before the Revolutionary War ended. In 1780 it provided that about eight thousand acres of escheated land in Kentucky would be vested in William Fleming and twelve other trustees as "a free donation from this Commonwealth, for the purpose of a public School or Seminary of learning." Three years later the number of trustees was enlarged to twenty-five and the institution styled Transylvania Seminary.

The organizational responsibilities for Transylvania Seminary were in the hands of the Reverend John Todd of the Hanover Presbytery in Virginia, his nephew Colonel John Todd, who was killed in the battle of Blue Licks, and Caleb Wallace. On November 10, 1783, thirteen Kentuckians, among whom were Benjamin Logan, Levi Todd, Samuel McDowell, John Bowman, Isaac Shelby, David Rice, Caleb Wallace, Walker Daniel, Robert Johnson, John Craig, James Speed, Christopher Greenup, and Willis Green, met at Crow's Station in Lincoln County and named a committee to seek subscriptions for additional funds. Not until 1785, however, did the trustees actually engage a teacher for the seminary.

Although Transylvania Seminary was slow in getting under way, it held forth a promise that citizens of Kentucky would have available an institution not unlike the College of William and Mary. Moreover, the charter of Transylvania Seminary was the prototype for Randolph Academy, established at Clarksburg, West Virginia, in 1787. The latter was founded to serve the Allegheny sections of Virginia and completed the triad of institutions of higher learning in the state.

Kentuckians, however, were more preoccupied with the pressing problems of land titles, defense, and political control than with cultural matters such as education and religion. No less than the framers of the Mayflower Compact or the Watauga Association, they understood the need for orderly and effective government. That recognition, combined with threats to their land claims, first pointed the way to cooperative endeavor among the Kentucky settlements and prompted Richard Henderson in 1775 to invite residents of Harrodsburg, Boiling Spring, and St. Asaph's to confer with him and the settlers at Boonesborough. At his suggestion, John Lythe, James Douglas, and Isaac Hite drew up a plan of government for the colony of Transylvania.

The alliance between Henderson and the Kentucky pioneers, which lasted about a year, could have been no more than a marriage of convenience. By 1775 Henderson's concept of a proprietary colony had become anachronistic, particularly to a generation of Americans brought up in the Revolutionary tradition. More significantly, perhaps, Kentuckians were justifiably dubious of Henderson's rights under the Treaty of Sycamore Shoals and questioned his ability to provide them protection against the Indians.

Circumstances may have forced Kentucky residents to reach an accommodation with Henderson, but there were no compelling reasons for them to devote any significant attention to a proposal in 1776 to create a new state to be known as Westsylvania. Its proponents, chief of whom apparently were George Croghan and disappointed Vandalia promoters, envisioned a state whose boundaries would have coincided closely with those of Vandalia. Among the arguments adduced in favor of the state were problems incident to the disputed jurisdiction of Virginia and Pennsylvania on the upper Ohio, difficulties arising out of the claims of Croghan and the Indiana Company, and the remoteness of most sections of the proposed state from existing seats of government. Since Westsylvania would have excluded the part of Kentucky west of the mouth of the Scioto River, it would not have embraced most of the lands claimed by Henderson or those marked off by Virginia speculators.

On the other hand, the philosophical arguments advanced in support of Westsylvania undoubtedly had as much appeal for Kentuckians as for residents of the Monongahela country, where most of the Westsylvania petitioners lived. In declaring that they were emigrants from "almost every Province in America" and that they had "imbibed the highest and most extensive Ideas of Liberty," they might have been speaking for Kentucky settlers. Even more akin to the thinking of Kentuckians was their assertion that their claims to their lands rested upon the "Laws of Nature and Nations" and their rejection of annexation by existing jurisdictions. Kentucky residents, however, had no need to concern themselves

117

with either the practical or the abstract reasoning set forth by the Westsylvania petitioners, since Congress had no intention of antagonizing both Pennsylvania and Virginia and of jeopardizing the unity of states whose independence was at best precarious.

The reluctance of Kentucky pioneers to place themselves under the banner of either Richard Henderson or of the Westsylvania advocates unquestionably derived from their conviction that their interests would best be served by recognizing the authority of Virginia over their remote settlements. Like other trans-Appalachian settlers, they had long since become accustomed to having their closest contacts with government at the county level. County governments provided such essential services as road building, licensing, maintaining vital statistics, recording of wills, deeds, and marriage and birth records, judicial functions, and defense structures. These services, along with validation of their land titles, were uppermost in the minds of Kentuckians when they dispatched George Rogers Clark and John Gabriel Jones to Williamsburg with their appeal to the Virginia legislature to sanction the formation of a new county.

In erecting a canopy of government over the Kentucky settlements through the creation of Kentucky County in December 1776, Virginia struck a severe blow at the claims not only of Henderson but also those of the Westsylvania promoters. In 1777 she followed this popular move by providing that any settler who had occupied western lands prior to June 1, 1776, would receive four hundred acres of land free. In order to prevent abuse of the system, however, settlers were required to have built a cabin or planted a crop of corn on the land. Recognizing the need for buffer settlements that might protect the western sections of the state, Virginia authorities also allowed those who arrived later to assume that they, too, might be permitted to take advantage of the "cultivation" law.

In 1779 Virginia enacted land legislation which had

almost incalculable effect upon Kentucky history. The right of preemption to four hundred acres of land was accorded to all who had settled in Kentucky before January 1, 1778. Those who had actually made improvements might claim an additional one thousand acres of adjoining land. Moreover, tracts might also be acquired by means of military bounties and treasury warrants, as well as by actual purchase. Settlers arriving between January 1, 1778, and January 1, 1779, could preempt four hundred acres by paying the established rate of forty pounds per hundred. Settlement warrants were for specific lands, but military and treasury warrants allowed the holder to select unpatented lands. All warrants were transferrable. Although the claims of the Loyal and Greenbrier companies were left intact, those of other speculative organizations, including the Ohio Company, the Westsylvania proponents, and Richard Henderson were mortally crippled.

To expedite the adjustment of western land claims, the new legislation divided the transmontane counties of Virginia into four districts. The Kentucky district, like the others, was served by four commissioners, who were forbidden by law to be residents of the district. Those appointed for the Kentucky district were William Fleming, Edmund Lynne, James Barbour, and Stephen Trigg. They held their first session at St. Asaph's on October 13, 1779. There Isaac Shelby presented the first claim. The commissioners held subsequent sessions at Harrodsburg, Boonesborough, Bryan's Station, and the Falls of the Ohio. About three thousand claims were laid before them during their first year of work.

Disillusionment with the Virginia land system came quickly for Kentuckians. As defenders of an exposed frontier, they believed that their rights should be given priority over those of absentee claimants who had contributed nothing to the defense of Kentucky. In this attitude they were no different from other pioneers of the trans-Appalachian region. The unwillingness of Virginia to alter her policy to enable those who had arrived after January 1, 1778, to acquire free lands probably contributed to a mounting wave of loyalism in Kentucky during the last years of the Revolutionary War.

The rapid growth of population and the constant danger from the Indians led to demands for the division of Kentucky County. By 1780 settlements were clustered in three sections of Kentucky. One was around the Falls of the Ohio, where several stations had sprung up after George Rogers Clark established Fort Nelson. The second center of settlement was northeast of the Kentucky River and included Lexington and Bryan's Station. The last, which embraced Harrodsburg and St. Asaph's, was south of the Kentucky. With the clerk of Kentucky County located at Harrodsburg and the court held at St. Asaph's, residents in the vicinity of the Falls of the Ohio and those northeast of the Kentucky River suffered great inconvenience. In a memorial reflecting typical frontier attitudes toward government, they asked the legislature to draw new county lines so that no citizen would be more than fifteen miles from his seat of government.

Virginia responded to western appeals by dividing Kentucky into three, the counties of Fayette, Jefferson, and Lincoln. Fayette County included the area north of a line running up the Kentucky River from its mouth to the head of its middle fork and thence in a south-easterly direction to the Washington County, Virginia, line. Jefferson County embraced the territory south of a line running along the Kentucky River from its mouth to Benson's Creek and thence by way of Hammond's Creek, the Town House Fork of Salt River, and the Green River to the Ohio. The remainder of Kentucky, within which were the settlements of Harrodsburg, Boonesborough, and St. Asaph's, became Lincoln County.

Simultaneous with the extension of county government was the founding of towns. In 1773 Thomas Bullitt, while on a surveying expedition, selected several town sites, one of which was that of Louisville, at the Falls of the Ohio. In 1779 Boonesborough became the first organized town in Kentucky, and in the following year Louisville, Washington, and Limestone, or Maysville, were established. Lexington, named for the battle in Massachusetts, was founded in 1781. First settled by Robert Patterson and twenty-nine others in 1779, Lexington became the transportation and commercial hub of central Kentucky and remained the leading center of the state until 1818, when Louisville, with its advantageous location on the Ohio River, began to supplant it as the chief metropolis of Kentucky.

Although the crudeness of a new frontier remained apparent in most parts of Kentucky throughout the eighteenth century, society in the Bluegrass region and the Louisville area had begun to take on aspects of maturity even before the end of the Revolutionary War. Political and social leadership rested with a landed aristocracy, which took root from the times of earliest settlement. Among those who accompanied James Harrod, for example, were Nathan Hammond, a wealthy Marylander, and Isaac Hite, the descendant of one of the prominent landholders of the Valley of Virginia. In addition to men who came from families who had exercised leadership on other frontiers, the aristocracy of Kentucky included those whose latent talents became apparent and whose wealth was acquired only after they moved west.

The creation of new counties and the growth of towns failed to ease a rising discontent with the government of Virginia, whose inadequate provisions for defense and unsatisfactory land policies ultimately produced an anti-Virginia element in Kentucky. Apparently directed from Virginia by Arthur Campbell, it gave rise to a separatist movement as early as 1779. After 1782 the new state forces had strong support from Virginia land companies. The separatists hoped that Virginia would willingly consent to statehood for Kentucky, but in case the Old Dominion proved uncooperative they favored simply proclaiming a new state and placing their fate in the hands of Congress.

Many of the men who regarded themselves as the natural leaders of Kentucky were relatively slow to embrace the cause of separation. Originally a pro-Virginia faction, they included a number of prominent surveyors, among whom were John Floyd, Robert Breckinridge, and Thomas and Humphrey Marshall. Nevertheless, they soon found that the great distance from Williamsburg, with the Appalachian Mountains intervening, constituted a major handicap to effective government in Kentucky. They objected to a tax of five shillings per hundred acres on lands patented under treasury warrants, which they viewed as lowering the value of all lands. In addition, they were distressed by the continuing Indian menace after the close of the Revolutionary War. In time, they, too, came to the conclusion that Kentuckians must chart their own future.

For residents of Kentucky the end of the Revolutionary War marked the dawn of a new era. Men whose energies and capabilities had been absorbed in carving homes from a wilderness and in defending their lives and possessions against an unrelenting enemy were now free to turn their attention to the building of a commonwealth of their own design. With its wealthy agrarian aristocracy and a conspicuous flair for leadership, Kentucky was ready, even before 1792, to take her place as the fifteenth state in the Union. Her pioneer period had been brief, but its influences were to prove enduring.

Bibliographical Note

THE MATERIALS, both primary and secondary, available to the student of the history of frontier Kentucky are extensive. Many of the former have been explored by careful scholars. My purpose in the present work has not been to reconnoiter the same ground that they have covered but rather to synthesize their most important findings and interpretations. By its very nature this work is constructed largely upon secondary sources. Since a major purpose is to set the history of frontier Kentucky in a broad context of regional and national development, it also follows that considerable reliance has been placed upon writings of a more general nature.

In this selected bibliography no effort has been made to be comprehensive. The reader interested in a detailed bibliography of pioneer Kentucky history is referred to J. Winston Coleman's excellent *A Bibliography of Kentucky History* (Lexington, Ky., 1949) and to the annual "Writings on Kentucky History," compiled by Jacqueline Bull and published in the *Register of the Kentucky Historical Society.*

The most useful general histories of the American frontier are Thomas D. Clark, *Frontier America: The Story of the Westward Movement* (New York, 1969), and Ray Allen Billington, *Westward Expansion: A History of the American Frontier* (New York, 1974). Still of importance is Frederick Jackson Turner's *The Frontier in American History* (New York, 1920), the pioneer work in the field.

Of regional studies, one of the earliest but still valuable is Theodore Roosevelt, *The Winning of the West,* 6 vols. (New York, 1889). Much briefer is the highly read-able work of Constance Lindsay Skinner, *Pioneers of the Old Southwest* (New Haven, Conn., 1921). More recent works include John A. Caruso's well-written *The Appalachian Frontier: America's First Surge Westward* (Indianapolis, Ind., 1959) and Francis S. Philbrick's *The Rise of the West, 1754–1830* (New York, 1965). More re-stricted in its focus but conceived in a regional perspec-tive is Otis K. Rice, *The Allegheny Frontier: West Virginia Beginnings, 1730–1830* (Lexington, Ky., 1970).

State histories of Kentucky which deal with the pio-neer period are numerous. Older accounts worthy of note include Temple Bodley, *History of Kentucky*, 4 vols. (Chicago, 1928); Charles Kerr, ed., *History of Kentucky*, 5 vols. (Chicago, 1922), of which the first volume, writ-ten by William Elsey Connelley and E. M. Coulter, per-tains to the period here considered; and Lewis and Richard H. Collins, *History of Kentucky*, 2 vols., rev. ed. (Covington, Ky., 1874). More useful for interpreta-tions are two works by Thomas D. Clark, *History of Kentucky* (Lexington, Ky., 1954) and *Kentucky: Land of Contrast* (New York, 1968). Robert S. Cotterill's *History of Pioneer Kentucky* (Cincinnati, Ohio, 1917) is more specifically concerned with the frontier era but needs correction at some points.

Studies dealing with the international conflict in the Ohio Valley are legion. Of older works, Francis Park-man, *A Half Century of Conflict*, 2 vols. (Boston, 1898), is still useful. Recent scholarly studies are Lawrence Henry Gipson, *The British Empire before the American Revolution*, 15 vols. (New York, 1936–1970), and How-ard H. Peckham, *The Colonial Wars, 1689–1763* (Chi-cago, 1964). W. J. Eccles has provided fresh interpreta-tions in two excellent volumes, *France in America* (New York, 1972) and *The Candian Frontier, 1534–1760* (New York, 1969). Of special value for the basis of the English claim to the Ohio Valley is Clarence Walworth Alvord and Lee Bidgood, *The First Explorations of the Trans-*

Allegheny Region by Virginians, 1650–1674 (Cleveland, Ohio, 1912). The role of Virginia in the French and Indian War is set forth in Hayes Baker-Crothers, *Virginia and the French and Indian War* (Chicago, 1928); Louis Knott Koontz, *The Virginia Frontier, 1754–1763* (Baltimore, Md., 1925); and Otis K. Rice, "The French and Indian War in West Virginia," *West Virginia History* 24 (January 1963). The Sandy River expedition is covered in detail in Otis K. Rice, "The Sandy Creek Expedition of 1756," *West Virginia History* 13 (October 1951). The most detailed account of the captivity of Mary Ingles is in John P. Hale, *Trans-Allegheny Pioneers: Historical Sketches of the First White Settlers West of the Alleghenies* (Charleston, W. Va., 1886).

General accounts of Pontiac's War are Francis Parkman, *The Conspiracy of Pontiac*, 2 vols. (Boston, 1910), and Howard H. Peckham, *Pontiac and the Indian Uprising* (Princeton, N.J., 1947). Peckham takes issue with Parkman's view that the war was a tightly organized undertaking and that Pontiac exercised decisive authority.

There are no comprehensive accounts of the Long Hunters. Useful brief summaries may be found in Harriet Simpson Arnow, *Seedtime on the Cumberland* (New York, 1960); Robert L. Kincaid, *The Wilderness Road* (Indianapolis, Ind., 1947); and Thomas D. Clark, *Kentucky: Land of Contrast*, already mentioned.

For the beginnings and later use of the Wilderness Road, the best accounts are William Allen Pusey, *The Wilderness Road to Kentucky* (New York, 1921), and Robert Kincaid, *The Wilderness Road*, already noted. A brief article is Thomas L. Connelly, "Gateway to Kentucky: The Wilderness Road, 1748–1792," *Register of the Kentucky Historical Society* 59 (April 1961). The exact route of the road, as well as of others into early Kentucky, is traced in Neal Owen Hammon's excellent article, "Early Roads into Kentucky," *Register of the Kentucky Historical Society* 68 (April 1970).

Two works are of prime importance to understanding

British policy with respect to the trans-Allegheny region between 1763 and 1775. They are Clarence Walworth Alvord, *The Mississippi Valley in British Politics*, 2 vols. (Cleveland, Ohio, 1917), and Jack M. Sosin, *Whitehall and the Wilderness: The Middle West in British Colonial Policy, 1760–1775* (Lincoln, Neb., 1961).

Writings on western land speculation are voluminous. The most significant general study is Thomas Perkins Abernethy, *Western Lands and the American Revolution* (New York, 1937). For the Ohio Company, essential works include Kenneth P. Bailey, *The Ohio Company of Virginia and the Westward Movement, 1748–1792: A Chapter in the History of the Colonial Frontier* (Glendale, Calif., 1939); Alfred P. James, *The Ohio Company: Its Inner History* (Pittsburgh, Pa., 1959); Kenneth P. Bailey, ed., *The Ohio Company Papers, 1753–1817* (Ann Arbor, Mich., 1947); and Lois Mulkearn, ed., *George Mercer Papers Relating to the Ohio Company of Virginia* (Pittsburgh, Pa., 1954). The best study of the Indiana Company is George E. Lewis, *The Indiana Company, 1763–1798: A Study in Eighteenth Century Frontier Land Speculation and Business Venture* (Glendale, Calif., 1941), and the most satisfactory account of the Loyal Company is Archibald Henderson, "Dr. Thomas Walker and the Loyal Land Company of Virginia," *American Antiquarian Society Proceedings*, n.s., 41 (1931). Corporate-sponsored explorations of Kentucky are documented in J. Stoddard Johnston, *First Explorations of Kentucky* (Louisville, Ky., 1898), which contains the journals of Christopher Gist of 1751 and Dr. Thomas Walker of 1750, and William M. Darlington, ed., *Christopher Gist's Journals* (Pittsburgh, Pa., 1893).

Three excellent studies of a biographical nature are Albert T. Volwiler, *George Croghan and the Westward Movement, 1741–1782* (Cleveland, Ohio, 1926); Nicholas B. Wainwright, *George Croghan: Wilderness Diplomat* (Chapel Hill, N.C., 1959); and John Richard Alden, *John Stuart and the Southern Colonial Frontier: A*

Study of Indian Relations, War, Trade, and Land Problems in the Southern Wilderness, 1754–1775 (Ann Arbor, Mich., 1944).

There are ample works on areas from which Kentucky settlers were drawn. Useful for the Holston and Watauga settlements are Samuel C. Williams, *Dawn of Tennessee Valley and Tennessee History* (Johnson City, Tenn., 1937), and briefer accounts in Thomas Perkins Abernethy, *From Frontier to Plantation in Tennessee* (Chapel Hill, N.C., 1932), and Stanley J. Folmsbee, Robert E. Corlew, and Enoch L. Mitchell, *History of Tennessee*, 2 vols. (New York, 1960). The standard biography of John Sevier is Carl S. Driver, *John Sevier: Pioneer of the Old Southwest* (Chapel Hill, N.C., 1932). There is no full-length study of James Robertson. Accounts of two important frontier settlements are James W. Hagy, "The Frontier at Castle's Woods, 1769–1786," *Virginia Magazine of History and Biography* 75 (October 1967), and William Allen Pusey, "The Location of Martin's Station, Virginia," *Mississippi Valley Historical Review* 15 (December 1928). For the Pennsylvania and West Virginia springboards to Kentucky, convenient accounts may be found in Solon J. Buck and Elizabeth Hawthorn Buck, *The Planting of Civilization in Western Pennsylvania* (Pittsburgh, Pa., 1939), and Otis K. Rice, *The Allegheny Frontier*, previously noted.

Although there remains much about Lord Dunmore and the situation in the Ohio Valley that is controversial, there are several works of merit for any understanding of the conditions there. Essential to that understanding is Reuben Gold Thwaites and Louise Phelps Kellogg, eds., *Documentary History of Dunmore's War, 1774* (Madison, Wis., 1905), a valuable collection of documents from the Draper Manuscripts. Useful interpretations are those of Randolph C. Downes in "Dunmore's War: An Interpretation," *Mississippi Valley Historical Review* 21 (December 1934), and *Council Fires on the Upper Ohio: A Narrative of Indian Affairs in the Upper*

Ohio Valley until 1795 (Pittsburgh, Pa., 1940). Special aspects of the conflict are treated in Percy B. Caley, "Lord Dunmore and the Pennsylvania-Virginia Boundary Dispute," *Western Pennsylvania History Magazine* 22 (June 1939), and Jack M. Sosin, "The British Indian Department and Dunmore's War," *Virginia Magazine of History and Biography* 74 (January 1966). A summary of events on the Ohio in the spring and summer of 1774 is in Otis K. Rice's introduction to John J. Jacob's *A Biographical Sketch of the Life of the Late Captain Michael Cresap* (Parsons, W. Va., 1970), a work originally published in 1826. The most detailed account of the battle of Point Pleasant is Virgil A. Lewis, *History of the Battle of Point Pleasant* (Charleston, W. Va., 1909).

Full-length studies of Kentucky pioneers include Charles Gano Talbert, *Benjamin Logan: Kentucky Frontiersman* (Lexington, Ky., 1962), the most scholarly biography of any pioneer Kentuckian, and the less satisfactory studies by Kathryn Harrod Mason, *James Harrod of Kentucky* (Baton Rouge, La., 1951), and Sylvia Wrobel and George Grider, *Isaac Shelby: Kentucky's First Governor and Hero of Three Wars* (Danville, Ky., 1974). Of the large number of works on Daniel Boone, the best is John Bakeless, *Daniel Boone* (New York, 1939). Other useful biographical works are Edna Kenton, *Simon Kenton: His Life and Period, 1755–1836* (Garden City, N.Y., 1930); James A. James, *The Life of George Rogers Clark* (Chicago, 1928); and Temple Bodley, *George Rogers Clark* (Philadelphia, 1957).

Of the numerous articles dealing with pioneer Kentuckians, mention should be made of Neal O. Hammon, "Captain Harrod's Company, 1774: A Reappraisal," *Register of the Kentucky Historical Society* 72 (July 1974); Lucien Beckner, "John Findley: The First Pathfinder of Kentucky," *History Quarterly* 1 (April 1927); James W. Hagy, "The First Attempt to Settle Kentucky: Boone in Virginia," *Filson Club History Quarterly* 44 (July 1970); and Anna M. Cartlidge, "Colonel John

Floyd: Reluctant Adventurer," *Register of the Kentucky Historical Society* 66 (October 1968). Three articles by Neal O. Hammon throw light on early surveying expeditions and the opening of the way to central Kentucky. They are "Fincastle Surveyors in the Bluegrass, 1774," *Register of the Kentucky Historical Society* 70 (October 1972); "The Fincastle Surveyors at the Falls of the Ohio, 1774," *Filson Club History Quarterly* 47 (January 1973); and "The First Trip to Boonesborough," *Filson Club History Quarterly* 45 (July 1971).

The role of the Transylvania Company in the settlement of Kentucky was first set forth in detail by Archibald Henderson in his *The Conquest of the Old Southwest* (New York, 1920), but the author's objectivity was marred by his esteem for Richard Henderson, his ancestor. More satisfactory, therefore, is William S. Lester, *The Transylvania Company* (Spencer, Ind., 1935).

For the Revolutionary War in Kentucky, one of the best places to begin is with a carefully edited four-volume series drawn from the Draper Manuscripts. Two of them, *The Revolution on the Upper Ohio, 1775–1777* (Madison, Wis., 1908) and *Frontier Defense on the Upper Ohio, 1777–1778* (Madison, Wis., 1912), were edited by Reuben Gold Thwaites and Louise Phelps Kellogg. The other two, edited by Kellogg, are *Frontier Advance on the Upper Ohio, 1778–1779* (Madison, Wis., 1916) and *Frontier Retreat on the Upper Ohio, 1779–1781* (Madison, Wis., 1917).

Among the many general secondary works on the war, those of special value for the Kentucky frontier include John R. Alden, *The American Revolution, 1775–1783* (New York, 1954) and *The South in the American Revolution, 1763–1789* (Baton Rouge, La., 1957); Willard M. Wallace, *The Appeal to Arms* (New York, 1951); and two other works of more restricted scope, Jack M. Sosin, *The Revolutionary Frontier, 1763–1783* (New York, 1967), and Dale Van Every, *A Company of Heroes: The American Frontier, 1775–1783* (New York, 1962).

Of interest for specific aspects of the war in Kentucky are George W. Ranck, *Boonesborough* (Louisville, Ky., 1901); Randolph C. Downes, "Indian War on the Upper Ohio, 1779–1782," *Western Pennsylvania History Magazine* 17 (June 1934); Charles G. Talbert, "Kentucky Invades Ohio—1780," *Register of the Kentucky Historical Society* 52 (October 1954), and "Kentucky Invades Ohio—1782," *Register of the Kentucky Historical Society* 53 (October 1955); and Patricia Watlington, "Discontent in Frontier Kentucky," *Register of the Kentucky Historical Society* 65 (April 1967).

The role of George Rogers Clark in the West is covered in James A. James, ed., *George Rogers Clark Papers, 1771–1784*, 2 vols. (Springfield, Ill., 1912–1926), and in two secondary accounts, Milo M. Quaife, *The Capture of Old Vincennes* (Indianapolis, Ind., 1927) and August Derleth, *Vincennes: Portal to the West* (Englewood Cliffs, N.J., 1968), as well as in biographies previously noted. In "To What Extent Was George Rogers Clark in Military Control of the Northwest at the Close of the Revolution?" *American Historical Association Annual Report for 1917* (Washington, D.C., 1920) and "The Northwest: Gift or Conquest?" *Indiana Magazine of History* 30 (March 1934), James A. James contends that Clark won the Northwest, but Clarence W. Alvord in "Virginia and the West: An Interpretation," *Mississippi Valley Historical Review* 3 (June 1916) disputes this claim. More recent assessments are John D. Barnhart, ed., *Henry Hamilton and George Rogers Clark in the American Revolution, with the Unpublished Journal of Lieut. Gov. Henry Hamilton* (Crawfordsville, Ind., 1951) and Barnhart's "A New Evaluation of Henry Hamilton and George Rogers Clark," *Mississippi Valley Historical Review* 37 (March 1951).

Information on cultural developments in frontier Kentucky is scattered. In addition to general histories, a valuable study of early education is Moses Edward Ligon, *A History of Public Education in Kentucky* (Lexington, Ky., 1942). For the beginnings of Transylvania College see James F. Hopkins, *The University of Kentucky: Origins and Early Years* (Lexington, Ky., 1951), and William Walter Jennings, *Transylvania: Pioneer University of the West* (New York, 1955).

General accounts of religious beginnings in Kentucky may be found in Walter Brownlow Posey, *Frontier Mission: A History of Religion West of the Southern Appalachians to 1861* (Lexington, Ky., 1966), an excellent work, and Robert H. Bishop, *An Outline of the History of the Church in the State of Kentucky* (Lexington, Ky., 1824). For the Baptists, useful works include John H. Spencer, *A History of Kentucky Baptists*, 2 vols. (Cincinnati, Ohio, 1885); John Taylor, *A History of Ten Baptist Churches* (Frankfort, Ky., 1823); George W. Ranck, *The Traveling Church* (Louisville, Ky., 1922); and two more recent studies of a general nature, Walter B. Posey, *The Baptist Church in the Lower Mississippi Valley, 1776–1845* (Lexington, Ky., 1957), and William Warren Sweet, ed., *Religion on the American Frontier: The Baptists, 1783–1830* (New York, 1931).

Methodist beginnings are traced in Albert H. Redford, *The History of Methodism in Kentucky*, 3 vols. (Nashville, Tenn., 1868–1870), and set in perspective in Walter B. Posey, *The Development of Methodism in the Old Southwest, 1783–1824* (Tuscaloosa, Ala., 1933), and William Warren Sweet, ed., *Religion on the American Frontier: The Methodists, 1783–1840* (Chicago, 1946). The foundations of Presbyterianism are set forth in Robert Davidson, *History of the Presbyterian Church in the State of Kentucky* (New York, 1847); Walter B. Posey, *The Presbyterian Church in the Old Southwest, 1778–1838* (Richmond, Va., 1952); Ernest T. Thompson, *Presbyterians in the South* (Richmond, Va., 1963); and William Warren Sweet, ed., *Religion on the American Frontier: The Presbyterians, 1783–1840* (New York, 1936). Useful for the planting of the Roman Catholic Church in Kentucky are Mary Ramona Mattingly, *The*

131

Catholic Church on the Kentucky Frontier, 1785–1812 (Washington, D.C., 1936), and Benjamin J. Webb, *The Centenary of Catholicity in Kentucky* (Louisville, Ky., 1884).

Political developments, at this early period often coupled with land problems and defense needs, are noted in most general histories of pioneer Kentucky. Especially useful are standard documentary collections such as William Waller Hening, comp., *The Statutes-at-Large: Being a Collection of All the Laws of Virginia from the First Session of the Legislature in the Year 1619*, 13 vols. (Richmond, Va., 1809–1823); William P. Palmer and others, eds., *Calendar of Virginia State Papers and Other Manuscripts*, 11 vols. (Richmond, Va., 1875–1893); and James R. Robertson, ed., *Petitions of the Early Inhabitants of Kentucky to the General Assembly of Virginia, 1769 to 1792* (Louisville, Ky., 1914). Other works which should be mentioned are George H. Alden, *New Governments West of the Alleghenies before 1780* (Madison, Wis., 1897); Patricia Watlington, *The Partisan Spirit: Kentucky Politics, 1779–1792* (Chapel Hill, N.C., 1974); and Robert M. Ireland, *County Courts in Antebellum Kentucky* (Lexington, Ky., 1972).

Index

Johnson, Sir William, 16–17, 52, 73, 86; and "Suffering Traders," 29, 30–33
Jones, John Gabriel, 82–85, 118

Kaskaskia, Ill., 96, 97
Kennedy, John, 90
Kenton, Simon, 28, 85, 97, 103
Kentucky Circuit, 114
Kentucky County, Va.: division of, 120; formation of, 84–85, 88, 118; militia of, 89, 91, 93, 96
Kentucky River, 31, 34, 44, 75, 95
King George's War, 3
Knox, James, 24, 55, 78

Lancaster, Treaty of, 7, 8
Land Law of 1779, 71, 111, 118–20
land speculation, 6, 9–10, 17, 29–35, 41, 43–49, 53–55, 59, 65, 70–71, 72–78, 80–85
Lawrenceburg, Ky., 50
Lee, Hancock, 70, 71
Lee, Thomas, 8
Lee, Willis, 71
Leestown, Ky., 70, 81, 95
Lewis, Andrew, 15, 32–33, 34, 87; role of, in Dunmore's War, 64, 65–69
Lewis, Charles, 66
Lewis, Jacob, 62
Lewis, John, 10
Lewis, Thomas, 70
Lexington, Ky., 95, 120, 121
Licking River, 31, 44, 70, 78, 95, 103
Lincoln County, Ky., 107, 108, 110, 120
Lindsay, Joseph, 109
Linn, Colonel William, 103–4, 105
Lochaber, Treaty of, 31, 34–35
Lochry, Archibald, 104
Logan (Mingo chief), 63
Logan, Ann, 90
Logan, Benjamin, 92, 94, 116; role of, in Kentucky militia, 85, 89,

90–91, 103–4, 105, 107–10; settlement of, 75–77, 80
Logan's Fort, 89, 90, 99. *See also* Logan's Station; Saint Asaph's
Logan's Station, 77, 82. *See also* Logan's Fort; Saint Asaph's
Long Hunters, 20–29, 35–36, 59
"Long Knives," 98
Louisa Company. *See* Transylvania Company
Louisville, Ky., 51, 104, 121
Loyal Company, 75, 119; corporate activity of, 29, 32, 45, 70–71; early claims of, 8, 10–11, 12, 17, 26
loyalism, 88, 120
Lunsford, Lewis, 113
Luttrell, John, 73, 75
Lynne, Edmund, 119
Lythe, John, 116

Mann, John, 51
Mansker, Kasper, 24, 27
Marin, sieur de (Captain Paul-Pierre de la Malgué), 6, 11
Marshall, Humphrey, 75–76, 122
Marshall, Thomas, 122
Martin, John, 78, 99
Martin, Joseph, 26, 42–43, 75
Martin's Station, 26, 43, 83, 95, 100, 103
Mason, George, 97
May, John, 115
Maysville, Ky., 28, 121
McAfee, George, 49, 50–51, 76
McAfee, James, 49, 50–51, 72, 76
McAfee, Robert, 49, 50–51, 72, 76
McAfee, William, 72
McAfee's Fort, 72, 95, 115
McClellan, John, 71, 89
McClellan's Station, 71, 95
McCoun, James, 49, 50–51
McDonald, Colonel Angus, 64
McDowell, Samuel, 65, 116
McGary, Hugh, 89, 108–9
McGee, Samuel, 72

McKee, Alexander, 92, 104, 106–8
McKinney, "Wildcat" John, 115
Mendenhall, James, 59–60
Mendenhall, Richard, 59–60
Mercer, George, 17
Mercer, Hugh, 54, 55
Miami, 4, 5, 94
military grants, 48, 50, 51, 52
military surveys, 48–52
military warrants, 48, 53
Mingo, 17, 63, 66, 87, 92, 93
Montague, Edward, 45
Montgomery, Captain John, 97
Mooney, James, 25–27
Moore, Thomas, 89
Morgan, George, 23, 48
Morgan, Colonel Zackquill, 92
Mount Sterling, Ky., 105
Murray, John (Earl of Dunmore),
    47, 48, 51, 73; land speculation
    of, 52–53; role of, in
    Revolutionary War, 86–87; war
    of, 49, 58–59, 62–69
Murray, William, 71

Nash, William, 55–56
Needham, James, 2
Neeley, Alexander, 27
Negro: presence of, in frontier
    Kentucky, 59–60, 75, 90, 105
Nelson, Governor William, 45
Neville, Captain John, 87
New River, 2
Nourse, James, 71

Occaneechi, 2
Oconostota (Cherokee chief), 74
Ogden, Benjamin, 114
Ohio Company, 29, 32, 119;
    activities of, 8–10, 17, 70–71
Ohio River, 1–2, 13, 19, 22, 23,
    104–5, 109; Falls of the, 51, 55,
    119, 120; Forks of the, 16
Ohio Valley: commercial rivalry in,
    3–5; corporate enterprise in,
    8–12, 17; fur trade in, 3, 5, 7;

international conflict in, 2–8,
    12–18; Iroquois claim of, 2–3
Ottawa, 17, 66, 87, 88, 92
Otter Creek, 78

Page, John, 73
Paris, Treaty of, 16, 110
Parker, William, 39
Patterson, Robert, 71, 109, 121
Patton, James, 47
Pauling, Henry, 65
Pineville, Ky., 22
Pitt, William, 4, 13
Pittsburgh, Treaty of, 87–88
Pluggy's Town, 93, 95
Point Pleasant, 95; battle of, 65–68,
    86, 111
Pontiac (Ottawa chief), 16, 17–
    18, 30
population, 78, 111, 120
Pottawattomi, 87
Powell Valley, 42–43
Preston, William, 47, 48, 52, 53,
    54, 56, 65
Pringle, John, 20, 35–36
Pringle, Samuel, 20, 35–36
Proclamation of 1763, 16, 20, 38,
    41; revised boundary of, 29–30,
    31, 32–34
proprietary rule: failure of, 80–81
Protestantism, 112–14

Randolph, Edmund, 10
Ray, William, 89
Reading, Joseph, 113
Regulator movement, 40
religious history, 42, 112–14
Revolutionary War, 85, 88–96,
    100–110
Rice, David, 113–14, 116
Richmond, Ky., 105
Robertson, Charles, 42
Robertson, James, 38, 39–40,
    41, 42
Robinson, David, 85
Robinson, James, 66

137

Twetty, Captain William, 75

Vanceburg, Ky., 50
Vandalia: proposed colony of, *44*,
   46–47, 117
Virginia, 7, 8, 65, 121–22;
   authority of, over Kentucky,
   80–81, 83, 84, 85, 87–88; charter
   of, of 1609, 1–2, 8; Continental
   Congress of, 84, 87–88, 93;
   General Assembly of, 71, 82, 83,
   84, 85, 96, 102, 109, 115; Land
   Law of, of 1779, 71, 111, 118–20;
   Valley of, 6–7, 8, 24, 38

Walden, Elisha, 21–22, 24, 26
Walker, Daniel, 116
Walker, Felix, 20, 42, 75
Walker, John, 87
Walker, Thomas, 10–11, 26, 32,
   34, 42–43, 87
Wallace, Caleb, 116
Walpole, Thomas, 43–45
Ward, Edward, 51
Warnsdorf, Charles, 51, 52, 55
Warriors Path, 2, 22, 24, 75

Washington, Augustine, 8
Washington, George, 12, 17, 37,
   60, 70–71
Washington, Ky., 121
Watauga Association, 42
Wayne, Anthony, 28, 110
Weiser, Conrad, 4
Westsylvania: proposed state of,
   44, 117–19
Wharton, Samuel, 30, 32, 43,
   45, 48
Whitley, Esther, 90
Whitley, William, 79, 80, 94, 97
Wilderness Road, 21, 26, 75, 76,
   78, 91
Williams, David, 54
Winchester, Ky., 4, 25
Wood, Abraham, 2
Wood, James, 87
Wormeley, Robert, 73
Wyandot, 87, 88, 92, 93, 102, 103,
   105, 106
Wythe, George, 97

Yeager, George, 28